Welcome to Hawaii!

This opening fold-out contains a general map of Hawaii to help you visualize the way the islands are explored in this guide, and 4 pages of valuable information, handy tips and useful addresses.

Discover Hawaii through 8 sections and 8 maps

A Oahu – Waikiki
B Oahu – Honolulu Historic Center
C Oahu – Suburban Honolulu and Eastern Oahu
D Oahu – North Shore
E Big Island – Hilo
F Big Island – Kamuela and Kailua-Kona
G Maui
H Lanai, Molokai, Kauai

For each section there is a double-page of addresses (restaurants – listed in ascending order of price – cafés, bars and stores), followed by a fold-out map for the relevant area with the essential places to see (indicated on the map by a star ★). These places are by no means all that Hawaii has to offer, but to us they are unmissable. The grid-referencing system (**A** B2) makes it easy for you to pinpoint addresses quickly on the map.

Transportation and hotels in Hawaii

The back fold-out consists of 5 pages of practical information that includes a selection of hotels.

Thematic index

Lists all the street names and sites featured in this guide.

ALTERNATIVE HAWAII

By helicopter
One of the best ways to view the outer islands' dramatic cliffs (especially Maui and Kauai) is by helicopter: *www.helicopters-hawaii.com* *www.bluehawaiian.com*
Latatudes and Adatudes: *www.ecomaui.com*

On horseback
A horseback tour is a great way to explore some of the islands' hard-to-reach or remote valleys:
Waipio on Horseback, Inc.
Tel. (877) 775-7291
www.mauihorses.com
www.kauaihorses.com
www.happytrailshawaii.com
www.konacowboy.com

KEIKI HULA DANCERS

KEY DATES

Hawaii is home to the only royal palace in America, and its people are justifiably proud of their storied past. The islands were settled by early Polynesian explorers (probably originally from Southeast Asia) who navigated their way across the Pacific in canoes some 2,000 years ago.
1778 Captain Cook lands at Kauai; dies at Kealakekua Bay in 1779.
1795 Kamehameha's army wins a decisive battle on Oahu.
1802 First known attempt to refine *ko* (sugarcane) into sugar.
1810 Kamehameha unites the Hawaiian islands and becomes King Kamehameha I, the first king. He dies in 1819.
1820 The first Christian missionaries arrive in Hawaii.
1820 Sugar plantations are established on the four main islands (Maui, Oahu, Big Island and Kauai) and quickly become the backbone of the Hawaiian economy.
1852 First immigrants brought in from China to work on the plantations.
1881 King David Kalakaua becomes first sovereign to circumnavigate the globe.
1893 After only two years on the throne Queen Liliuokalani (Kalakaua's sister) is overthrown and kept under house arrest.
1898 Hawaii annexed.
1936 First passenger plane flies from Mainland USA to Hawaii.
1959 Hawaii granted statehood.

Early Sep: Aloha Week Festival, islandwide.
Late Sep: Molokai Music Festival, Meyer Sugar Mill (Molokai).
October
Early Oct: Ironman Triathlon World Championship, Kailua (Big Island).
Late Oct: Mokihana Festival, hula and crafts (Kauai).
November
Late Oct-early Nov: Kona Coffee Cultural Festival, South Kona (Big Island).
Mid-Nov: Hawaii International Film Festival, Honolulu (Oahu).
Mid-Nov through mid-Dec: Triple Crown of Surfing, North Shore locations (Oahu). **Mid-Nov:** PGA Grand Slam golf tournament, Po'ipu (Kauai).
December
Dec 25: Christmas Day, statewide holiday; Aloha Bowl Football Classic, Honolulu (Oahu).

EATING OUT

Meal times
Because the state is an early-to-bed, early-to-rise place (many schools hold their first classes at 7.30am), restaurants and casual eateries alike open their doors early; unfortunately it also means the last dinnertime seating in most restaurants is around 9.30pm or, if you're lucky, 10pm.

Eating habits
Hawaiians love food; you can eat very well at very reasonable prices in small restaurants throughout the islands. There are also a number of gourmet restaurants and renowned chefs often found in top-class hotels. Hawaii's cuisine is varied and creative, but Hawaii's real culinaria franca is what's referred to as 'local', a starch-heavy, irresistible soul-food-like comfort cuisine. Here are some of its most popular dishes:
Plate lunch: two scoops of white rice, a scoop of macaroni salad, a mound of pale shredded cabbage, and your choice of meat – everything from teriyaki chicken and *kalbi* to grilled *mahimahi* and *laulau*.
Chicken long rice: clear noodles and shredded chicken simmered in chicken broth and topped with green onions.
Oxtail soup: Hawaii's version is a thick, meaty, opaque broth chunky with rice, peanuts, freshly grated ginger, shiitake mushrooms, heaps of cilantro, strips of cabbage, and, of course, small boulders of rich, fatty oxtail meat still on the bone. Some people add a dash of *shoyu* (soy sauce) to the broth.
Laulau: pork and butterfish (black cod), steamed inside

STATE PROFILE

• 50th of the United States • The six main Hawaiian islands are: Kauai, Oahu, Molokai, Lanai, Maui and Hawaii (known as the Big Island) • Combined area of 6,470 sq. miles (Big Island alone is 4,028 sq. miles) • 1.21 million inhabitants (82 percent live on Oahu) • 7 million tourists every year • Highest peak: Mauna Kea on Big Island: 13,796 ft • Over 80 golf courses • Warm winter (78°F); warm summer (83°F) • Time difference: New York + 5 hrs; GMT – 8 hrs • Currency: the US$.

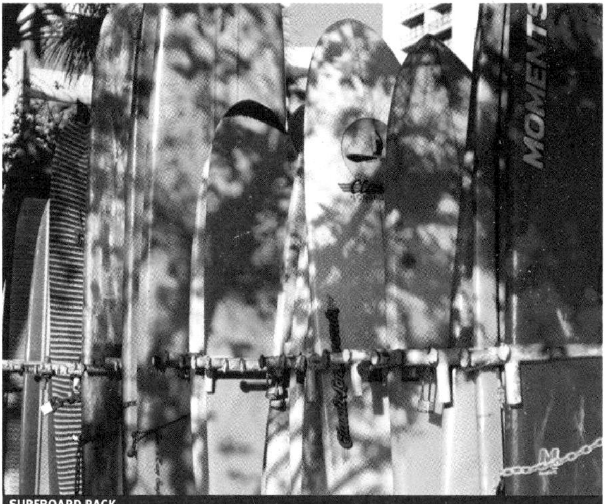
MOMENTS
SURFBOARD RACK

TOURIST INFO

Hawaii Visitors and Convention Bureau
→ *2270 Kalakaua Ave, 8th Floor, Honolulu Tel. (808) 923-1811 Fax (808) 924-0290 www.gohawaii.com*

Pharmacies
There are no 24-hour pharmacies in Hawaii. Long's Drugstores (with multiple locations in Waikiki and one in Ala Moana) is the islands' best-represented drugstore chain.

TELEPHONE

UK to Hawaii
→ *00 + 1 (USA) + 808 (state of Hawaii) + number*
Hawaii to the UK
→ *011 + 44 (UK) + number without initial 0*
Within the state
→ *Dial 808 when calling from one island to another.*

Useful numbers
Police, ambulance and fire emergencies: *911*
International operator: *0*

FORMALITIES

Are the same as if you were going to mainland United States.
Consular Information Unit
→ *24 Grosvenor Square, W1 Tel. 09055 444 546 Mon-Fri 8am–8pm (visa services) www.usembassy.org.uk*

OPENING HOURS

Banks, official offices
→ *Mon-Fri 8am–3pm (until 4/5pm for offices).*
Stores
→ *Generally: daily 9/10am to at least 6pm (shorter hours on Sun). Shopping malls: Mon-Sat 9am–9pm; Sun 10am–5pm.*
Public holidays
→ *Jan 1, March 26, May 1, June 11, 3rd Fri in Aug.*

CALENDAR

January-February
3rd week in Jan–3rd week in Feb: Chinese New Year. Celebrations, lion dances and fireworks statewide.
1st weekend in Feb: Punahou School Carnival, Honolulu (Oahu).
March
Early March: Whale Fest Week, Lahaina (Maui).
March 26: Prince Kuhio Day, public holiday statewide.
March/April
Easter Sunday: start of the one-week Merrie Monarch Festival: the hula event of the year (Big Island).
May
May 1: Lei Day: public holiday with statewide celebrations. Late May: Maui Jazz Festival (Maui).
June
June 11: Kamehameha Day, public holiday with statewide celebrations. A parade runs through downtown Honolulu toward Waikiki (Oahu).
Mid-June: Maui Film Festival, Wailea (Maui).
Late June: King Kamehameha Hula Festival, Honolulu (Oahu).
July
Mid-July: Hawaii International Jazz Festival, Honolulu (Oahu); Quicksilver Cup windsurfing competition, Kanaha Beach (Maui).
Mid-July: Slack Key Festival, Hilo (Big Island).
Late July: Prince Lot Hula Festival, Moanalua Gardens (Oahu).
August
Mid-Aug: *O-bon* festival, at Buddhist temples statewide. 3rd Friday in Aug: Admission Day, statewide public holiday.
September
Early Sep: Parker Ranch Rodeo, Kamuela (Big Island).

Welcome to Hawaii!

- A Oahu – Waikiki
- B Oahu – Honolulu Historic Center
- C Oahu – Suburban Honolulu and Eastern Oahu
- D Oahu – North Shore
- E Big Island – Hilo
- F Big Island – Kamuela and Kailua-Kona
- G Maui
- H Lanai, Molokai, Kauai

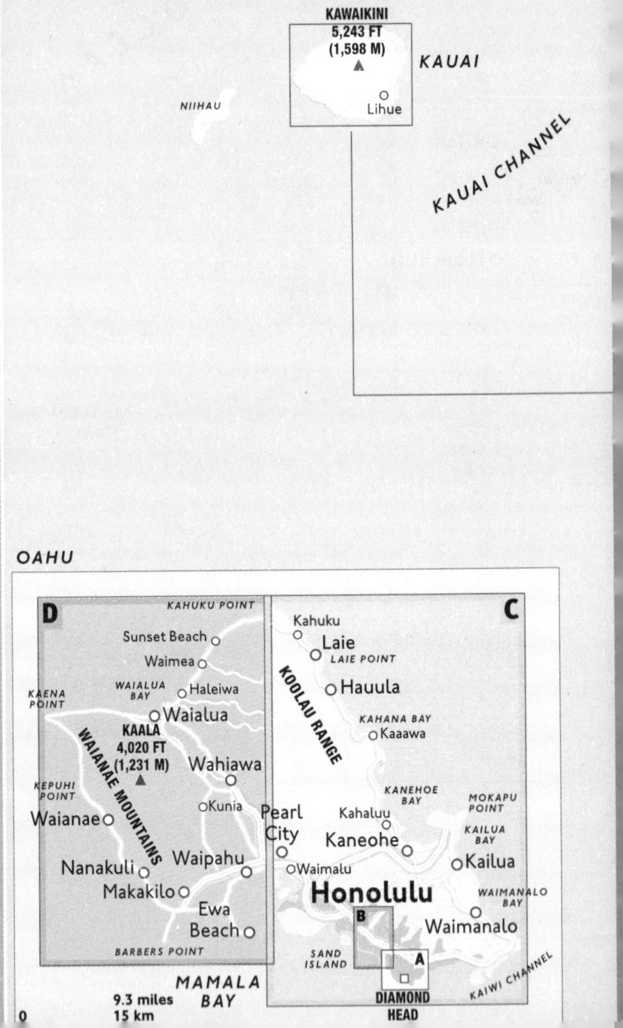

KAWAIKINI
5,243 FT
(1,598 M)
KAUAI
NIIHAU
Lihue
KAUAI CHANNEL
OAHU
D
C
KAHUKU POINT
Sunset Beach
Waimea
WAIALUA BAY
Haleiwa
KAENA POINT
Waialua
KAALA
4,020 FT
(1,231 M)
WAIANAE MOUNTAINS
Wahiawa
KEPUHI POINT
Waianae
Kunia
Pearl City
Nanakuli
Waipahu
Makakilo
Ewa Beach
BARBERS POINT
MAMALA BAY
Kahuku
Laie
LAIE POINT
KOOLAU RANGE
Hauula
KAHANA BAY
Kaaawa
KANEHOE BAY
MOKAPU POINT
Kahaluu
KAILUA BAY
Kaneohe
Kailua
Waimalu
Honolulu
WAIMANALO BAY
B
Waimanalo
SAND ISLAND
A
DIAMOND HEAD
KAIWI CHANNEL
0
9.3 miles
15 km

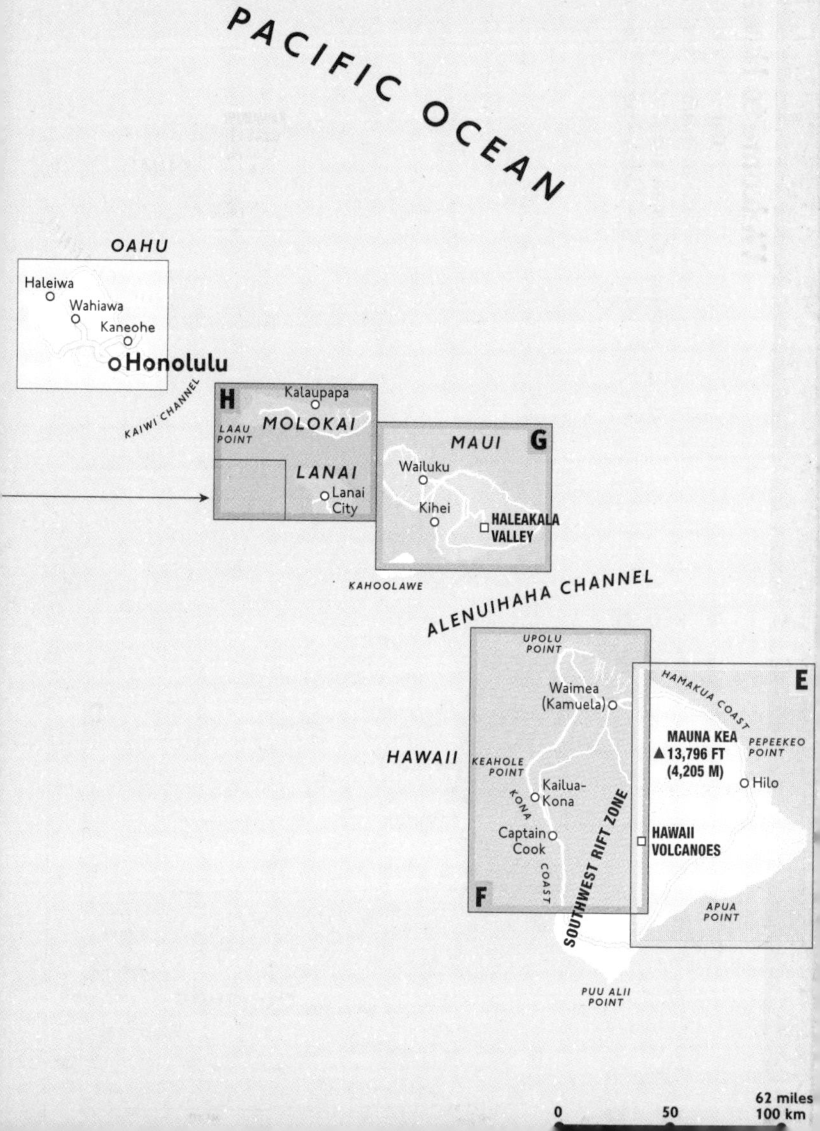

PACIFIC OCEAN
OAHU
Haleiwa
Wahiawa
Kaneohe
Honolulu
KAIWI CHANNEL
H
Kalaupapa
LAAU POINT
MOLOKAI
LANAI
Lanai City
MAUI
G
Wailuku
Kihei
HALEAKALA VALLEY
KAHOOLAWE
ALENUIHAHA CHANNEL
UPOLU POINT
HAMAKUA COAST
E
Waimea (Kamuela)
MAUNA KEA 13,796 FT (4,205 M)
PEPEEKEO POINT
HAWAII
KEAHOLE POINT
Kailua-Kona
KONA COAST
Hilo
Captain Cook
HAWAII VOLCANOES
SOUTHWEST RIFT ZONE
F
APUA POINT
PUU ALII POINT
0
50
62 miles
100 km

STRANDS OF LEIS

angelic singing voice and had died in his thirties of obesity).

Radio stations

Two of the best music stations in Honolulu, 100.3 FM and 105.1, play a mix of old-style slack-key guitar music and newer, reggae-tinged modern beats. Other good stations are 93.5 and 107.3 on Maui; 93.5 on Kauai; 94.7 on the Big Island (Hilo).

Classical music

Honolulu has a symphony as well as an opera company. For schedules and details, check a listings guide, such as the *Honolulu Weekly*, or go to *www.honolulusymphony.com* or *hawaiiopera.org*.

Nightlife

Most bars are either heavily local or strictly tourist. Many hotels such as the Halekulani, the W, and the Ilikai, on the edge of Waikiki, maintain bars that draw a wide cross-section of visitors and locals alike. Many of these bars offer an added bonus: live entertainment by some of the best Hawaiian musicians around, such as Robert Cazimero, Hapa and Aunty Genoa Keawe, an octogenarian falsetto singer who still belts it out once a week. You can listen to a national treasure for the price of a few drinks.

OCEAN SPORTS

Hawaii is the official birth-place of surfing (a statue of Duke Kahanamoku, the father of modern surfing, stands watch over Waikiki Beach), and there are all manner of surfing, windsurfing, parasailing, kayaking, waterskiing, sailing and scuba schools. Stands near the Kahanamoku statue (on Waikiki Beach heading toward Diamond Head) rent surfboards for around $10. There are also surfing lessons for around $40/hr. Or take a tutorial with a pro from Hans Hedemann Surf School (around $130/2 hrs; 924-7778) in either Waikiki or on the North Shore. They also offer bodyboarding and kayaking lessons. Most hotels also have a watersports activities director on hand, or can connect you with a reputable instructor.

WWW.

→ *gohawaii.com*
Everything you need to know about the islands.
→ *hawaii.gov/tourism/*
Hawaiian Tourist Authority.
→ *hawaii.net*
→ *aloha-hawaii.com*
→ *alternative-hawaii.com*

'PIDGIN'

Hawaii has two official languages: English and Hawaiian. A decade or so ago, finding someone who spoke Hawaiian was a near-impossible task. Now, new Hawaiian-language immersion schools are insuring that the next generation of *keiki* (kids) will be fluent in the islands' mothertongue. However Hawaii's true lingua franca is pidgin, a colorful creole of a language that everyone in the islands speaks with some level of fluency. Pidgin – a mishmash of English, Hawaiian, Chinese, Japanese, Tagalog, Samoan, Portugese and Korean – was developed in the 19th-century pineapple and sugar plantations by the Asian laborers who created the islands' current ethnic polyglot. The dialect is particularly Japanese-heavy, which makes sense: Japanese account for Hawaii's single largest Asian ethnicity, and visitors from Japan will notice that everyone in the islands, whether haole or Hawaiian, sprinkles their speech with the language, whether complaining about how *atsui* (hot) it is, or asking for some extra *shoyu* (soy sauce). But mostly, visitors notice pidgin's distinct, sing songy rhythm, which makes everyone sound friendly and approachable (even when they're not).

MAKING POI

BEACHES

All of Hawaii's beaches – except those run on military soil – are open to the public, including those in front of resorts and private homes. Most (but not all) have lifeguards on duty seven days a week, usually from sunup to sundown. Make sure to pay close attention to any signs or red flags staked out by the lifeguard; they'll tell you whether the undertow is strong or man-o-wars (a lovely, silvery blue, jellyfish-like creature with an intense, burning sting) have been spotted in the water.

Best Kine
REAL
Matsumoto
SHAVE ICE
North Shore Haleiwa,
No-28
MATSUMOTO SHAVE ICE

NENE, HAWAII'S NATIONAL BIRD

a tightly bound package of ti leaves.
Pipikaula: peppery jerked beef.
Chopsteak: a *paniolo* favorite: ribbons of skirt steak fried with sweet Maui onions and served over rice.
Kalua pig: juicy, pit-cooked shredded pork with a distinctive, smoky flavor.
Lomilomi salmon: refreshing salad of diced red onions, tomatoes, cilantro, garlic and small cubes of bright-pink salmon.
Manapua: the Chinese call it *bao*. A cushiony white baked or steamed dumpling, filled, in Hawaii, with curry chicken, turkey meat, vegetables and hot dogs.
Poi: not a tourist favorite, but a must-try, poi is mashed taro root, with a dull aubergine color and the consistency of a thick paste; sticky and very filling, it can be eaten either fresh or slightly fermented, topped with sugar or salt.
Spam musubi: the enduring appeal of Hawaii's most beloved fast food – a thick slab of rice topped with a slice of charred Spam luncheon meat and wrapped in nori (dried sheet seaweed) – has befuddled generations of tourists. It's best not to even try to understand it.

Snacks

Hawaii loves to snack. Some snacks (most Asian-influenced) you'll encounter in the drugstore are:
Boiled peanuts: they come refrigerated or fresh; the meat is easily plucked from its damp shell and has an oddly appealing cardboardy taste.
Crack seed: a catchall name for various pickled or cured fruits (mango, plum, cherry seeds, lychee), which are available either wet or dry and have a distinctive, powerful, sweet-and-sour anise-like taste.
Kaki mochi: crunchy, salty rice cracker better known as *arare*.
Shoyu peanut: peanuts surrounded by a hard shoyu shell.
Squid and cuttlefish legs: you can get them dried or wet (with a chili-and-sesame paste).

Short glossary

Ahi: yellowfin tuna
Azuki beans: starchy, semi-sweet red Japanese beans
Lilikoi: passion fruit
Limu: seaweed
Luau: a culinary feast nowadays mostly staged for tourists as the real ones are family affairs to which outsiders are not invited
Mahimahi: dolphin fish
Ohelo: yellow or red berry similar to the cranberry
Ono: butterfish (black cod)
Opae: shrimp
Opakapaka: snapper (usually red or pink)
Opihi: limpet
Poke: raw marinated fish
Pupus: appetizers
Saimin: Japanese noodle
Shave ice: finely ground ice drenched in sugary flavored syrup

Tipping

A standard 15 to 20 percent of the bill.

ENTERTAINMENT

Movies

For mainstream movies, check listings in the local newspaper. The Honolulu Academy of Arts and the University of Hawaii show alternative and art-house films.

Music

The guitar's distinctive twang, the chill-inducing chants, the aching falsetto songs... to love Hawaii is to love Hawaiian music. The islands' most beloved son is the late Israel Kamakawiwoole, a sort of David Beckham figure in Hawaii (if Beckham had an

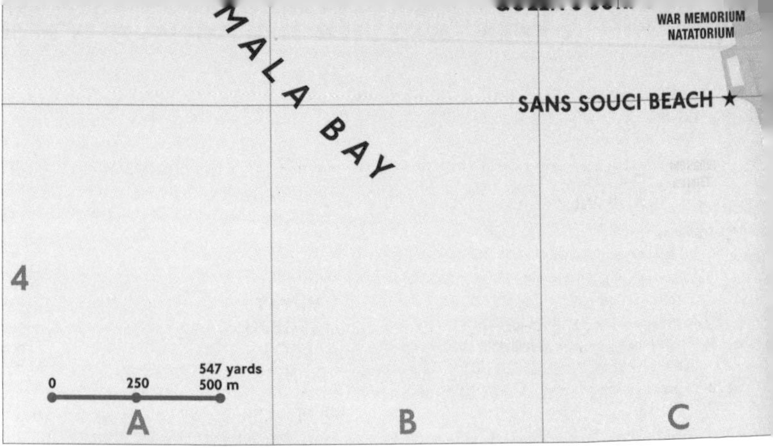

WAR MEMORIUM
NATATORIUM
MALA BAY
SANS SOUCI BEACH ★
4
0
250
547 yards
500 m
A
B
C

KAPIOLANI PARK

DIAMOND HEAD AND WAIKIKI BEACHES

HONOLULU ZOO

Ala Moana Beach Park and Magic Island Beach Park (**A** west of A1)
These two beaches are favorites with tourists and locals alike. On weekends, families flock to Ala Moana Beach Park for picnics, barbecues and birthday parties. But the water's cleaner (and the beach less crowded) at nearby Magic Island, a small artificial bay at the end of a small park dotted with enchanting flowering trees.

Waikiki Beaches (**A** B-C)
Waikiki, Fort DeRussy, Queen's Surf, Sans Souci
Each of the beaches on Hawaii's most famous shoreline has its own personality. The ones nearest the big hotels, Fort DeRussy and Waikiki, are fun to visit as cultural reference points, but the water is oily and the beach crowded. Closer to Diamond Head, the less frenetic Queen's Surf (which is a popular gay beach), Sans Souci and Kaimana, local favorites all, are great for swimming.

Doris Duke House/ Islamic Art Center
(**A** east of F4)
→ 4055 Papu Circle Tel. 734-1941 Wed-Sat 8.30am–1.30pm (last tour begins). Book as far ahead as possible; check www.honoluluacademy.org
The billionaire heiress Doris Duke, one of Hawaii's most famous and reclusive residents, was a renowned collector of Middle Eastern art, much of which was displayed at Shangri La, her sumptuous (but completely inaccessible) Diamond Head hideaway. In her will, Duke, who died in 1993, allowed for the creation of the Doris Duke Foundation for Islamic Art, and last year, Shangri La, with its 3,500-plus collection of every kind of decorative or fine Middle Eastern art imaginable, opened to the public or a limited basis. The onl way to see Shangri La ir person is through an excellent tour run by the Honolulu Academy of A which administers the foundation. Beware, the house is not air conditioned and can be very warm and reservat can be impossible to co by: a trip here is a deca feast for the senses and locals have been waitin see the inside of Shang La for years.

Waikiki Shell and Kapiolani Park (**A** D3)
→ 2805 Monsarrat Ave Tel. 924-8934

SANS SOUCI BEACH

WAIKIKI BEACH

DORIS DUKE HOUS

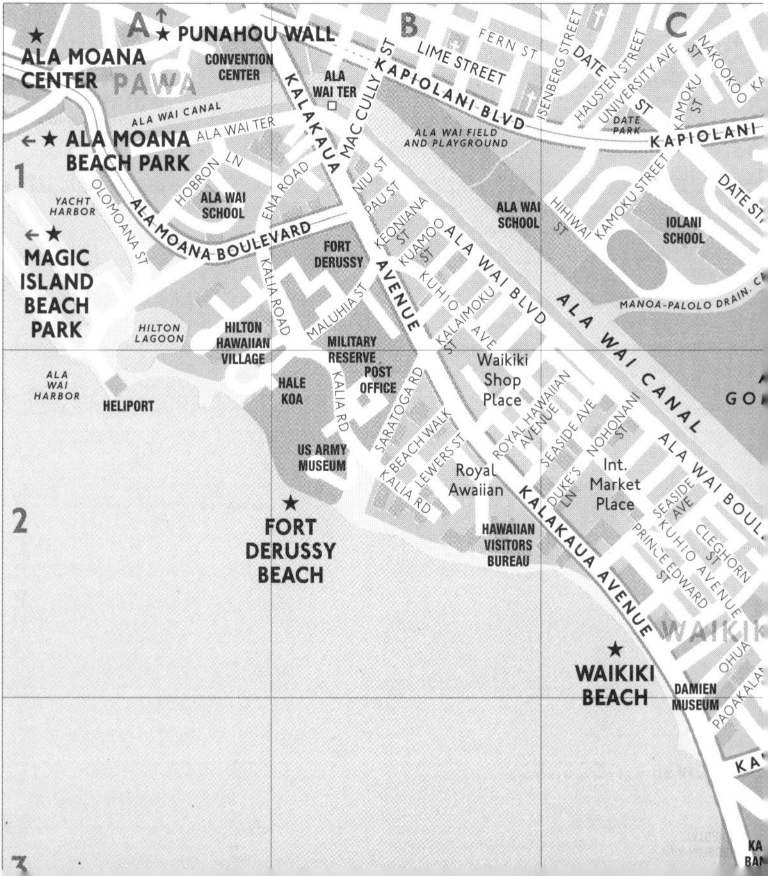
PUNAHOU WALL
ALA MOANA CENTER
CONVENTION CENTER
ALA WAI TER
ALA WAI CANAL
ALA MOANA BEACH PARK
YACHT HARBOR
ALA WAI SCHOOL
ALA MOANA BOULEVARD
MAGIC ISLAND BEACH PARK
FORT DERUSSY
HILTON LAGOON
HILTON HAWAIIAN VILLAGE
MILITARY RESERVE
ALA WAI HARBOR
HELIPORT
HALE KOA
POST OFFICE
US ARMY MUSEUM
FORT DERUSSY BEACH
KALAKAUA AVENUE
MAC CULLY ST
KAPIOLANI BLVD
LIME STREET
FERN ST
ISENBERG STREET
DATE ST
HAUSTEN STREET
UNIVERSITY AVE
KAMOKU ST
NAKOOKOO ST
DATE PARK
ALA WAI FIELD AND PLAYGROUND
ALA WAI SCHOOL
IOLANI SCHOOL
KAMOKU STREET
HIHIWAI ST
MANOA-PALOLO DRAIN
ALA WAI BLVD
ALA WAI CANAL
Waikiki Shop Place
Royal Awaiian
Int. Market Place
HAWAIIAN VISITORS BUREAU
WAIKIKI BEACH
DAMIEN MUSEUM
KALIA ROAD
ENA ROAD
HOBRON LN
OLOMOANA ST
NIU ST
PAU ST
KEONIANA ST
KUAMOO ST
KUHIO AVE
KALAIMOKU ST
MALUHIA ST
SARATOGA RD
BEACH WALK
LEWERS ST
ROYAL HAWAIIAN AVENUE
SEASIDE AVE
NOHONANI ST
DUKE'S LN
PRINCE EDWARD ST
CLEGHORN ST
OHUA
PAOAKALANI

Gloriously tacky, unapologetically mercenary and matter-of-factly tourist-friendly, Waikiki was, for many years, all visitors knew of Honolulu. In the 1990s, the tide turned against this eclectic, electric neighborhood, which was deemed too artificial, too contrived, too outré. But recently, Waikiki has experienced a second wave of interest and has found new fans for its unique brand of retro charm. But the unconvinced shouldn't dismiss the neighborhood so quickly – for every chain store or overcrowded beach, there's an undiscovered gem of a store selling wondrous baubles and a stretch of glittering, clean white sand.

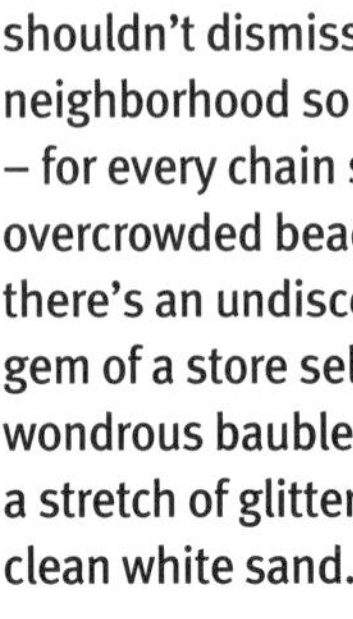

HULA'S BAR

GARAKUTA-DO

RESTAURANTS

Ono Hawaiian Foods (**A** D2)
→ *726 Kapahulu Ave*
Tel. 737-2275
Mon-Sat 11am–7.45pm
A line of tourists and locals forms outside this Hawaiian hole-in-the-wall every night. They come for *kalua* pig (shredded salted pork), *laulau* (fish, and pork smoked in ti leaves), grilled butterfish (black cod), poi (mashed taro root), and *haupia*, a gently sweet gelatinous coconut pudding.
À la carte $12.

Izakaya Nonbei (**A** E1)
→ *3108 Olu St*
Tel. 734-5573
Daily 5.30pm–midnight
Waikiki crooner Don Ho is a part owner of this down-home, smoky Japanese country-style spot usually packed with locals. Don't miss *tapas*-style Japanese food (smoked octopus, miso-grilled mackerel) rarely found in other Japanese restaurants. À la carte $13.

Wasabi Bistro (**A** D1)
→ *1006 Kapahulu Ave*
Tel. 735-2800 Daily 11.30am–2pm, 5.30–10pm
Hip, urbane Japanese and locals have made this sushi joint a favorite among young people; the carefully arranged platters of sushi are as sleek, chic and spare as the patrons nibbling at them.
À la carte $25.

Sam Choy's (**A** D2)
→ *449 Kapahulu Ave*
Tel. 732-8645 Mon-Thu 5.30–9pm (5pm Fri-Sun)
Sam Choy's is famous for fresh ingredients (fish especially), exuberance (in both service and cuisine) and jaw-droppingly enormous portions.
A fat fillet of mahi comes balanced atop a cake of sticky short-grain rice and baby bok choy, festooned with fruit and vegetable confetti. À la carte $27.

Kyo-ya (**A** B1)
→ *2057 Kalakaua Ave*
Tel. 947-3911 Mon-Sat 11am–1.30pm, 5.30–9pm
One of the island's most venerable Japanese restaurants, Kyo-ya morphed in the early 1990s from a modest eatery into an elegant Waikiki institution. Lunch here – the $18 special is a beautifully composed paean to the season's ingredients. À la carte $27.

La Mer at the Halekulani (**A** B2)
→ *2199 Kalia Rd*
Tel. 923-2311 Daily 6–10pm
The flavorful cuisine at this

ALA MOANA CENTER

BAILEY'S ANTIQUES

WORKSPACE

gracious and elegant restaurant – Pacific Rim with a touch of Provençal – is superb and the dessert list is famous. À la carte $28.

CAFÉS, BARS

Wailana Coffee House (**A** A1)
→ *1860 Ala Moana Blvd*
Tel. 955-1764 Daily 24 hrs
This Honolulu institution, situated at the lip of brightly lit Waikiki, is ideal for kitsch value, people-watching and atmosphere. Stop for a coffee and sandwich. $6.

Diamond Head Grill at the W (**A** C3)
→ *2885 Kalakaua Ave*
Tel. 922-3734
Sun-Thu 5.30pm–12.30am (2am Fri-Sat)
Crammed with hip young locals and hip young tourists, this atmospheric bar has a beautiful, diverse crowd and a buzzy, eager vibe. It often hosts jazz trios, but people-watching is usually entertainment enough.

Lewers Lounge at the Halekulani (**A** B2)
→ *2199 Kalia Rd*
Tel. 923-2311
Daily 8.30pm–1am
A gracious, romantic throwback of a bar in elegant, peaceful surroundings, a visit to Lewers feels like a step out of place and time – it's a great place for a sophisticated drink away from the neighborhood's din and one of the city's few upscale lounges. (The bar is housed in the Halekulani, the islands' most venerable hotel.) Live jazz every night.

Hula's Bar and Lei Stand (**A** C3)
→ *134 Kapahulu Ave*
Tel. 923-0669
Daily 10am–2am
A Waikiki favorite that is also one of Honolulu's only gay bars, where you can also shoot pool, or dance the night away.

SHOPPING

Ala Moana Center (**A** A1)
→ *Most stores: 10am–9pm*
Hawaii's largest shopping center is multilevel, open-air and offers something for every taste, from T&C Surf with boards and witty, graphic T-shirts; to the sophisticated aloha shirts of Reyn Spooner Hawaii businessmen wear instead of suits; also Neiman Marcus, Bottega Veneta, Louis Vuitton and Prada outposts.

Avanti Waikiki (**A** B2)
→ *2164 Kalakaua Ave*
Tel. 924-1688
Daily 9am–11pm
This store is a riot of colors: red surfboard-printed aloha shirts, blue-and-salmon skirts and black dresses with a bird of paradise pattern. Avanti specializes in high-quality silks printed in China with retro patterns from the 1940s and 1950s.

Garakuta-do (**A** B1)
→ *1833 Kalakaua Ave*
Tel. 955-2099 Tue-Sat 10am–6pm (4pm Sun)
This Japanese antique store, with its tansu chests, bolts of kimono silk, hand-wrought textiles and heaps of glittering, gold-threaded obis, is like walking into a cabinet of wonders. There are gifts and collectibles in all price ranges.

Bernard Hurtig (**A** A1)
→ *2005 Kalia Rd, Hilton Hawaiian Village,*
Tel. 947-9399
Daily 9am–10pm
This Hawaii mainstay jeweler dabbles in various Japanese antiquities (Imariware and netsuke, mostly), but it also offers a wide selection of Hawaii's distinctive heirloom jewelry.

Workspace (**A** F1)
→ *3624 Waialae Ave*
Tel. 732-2300 Thu-Sat noon–6pm (4pm Sun)
Founded as a collective by a group of young artists, this small, energetic gallery has the island's contemporary art scene cornered. The gallery hosts frequent well-curated and attended group and individual shows; there's lots of affordable pieces available – etchings, drawings and sculptures.

Bailey's Antiques (**A** D2)
→ *517 Kapahulu Ave*
Tel. 734-7628
Daily 10am–6pm

Hawaii Antique Center (**A** D1)
→ *932 Kapahulu Ave*
Tel. 734-6222
Tue-Sat 11am–5pm
No visit to Honolulu would be complete without a visit to these two stores, both of which celebrate Hawaii's ingeniously tacky, brightly plastic pre-statehood days. Bailey's is the place for jiggly-hipped hula-girl dolls and vintage aloha shirts, and the Hawaii Antique Center has a handsome collection of vintage rattan furniture, all reupholstered in tropical barkcloth fabric.

GARDEN

OUTSIDE

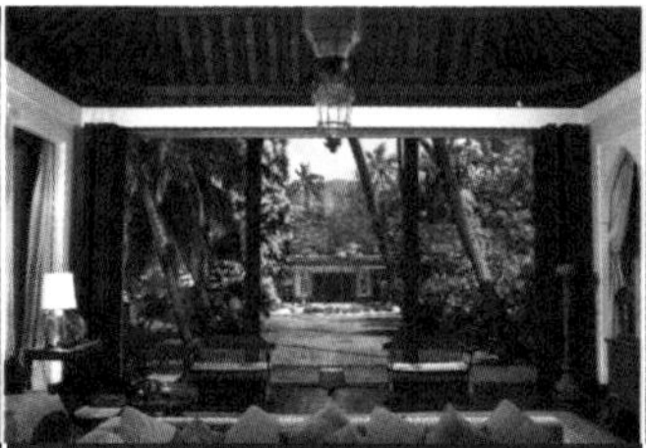
THE PLAYHOUSE

THE TURKISH ROOM

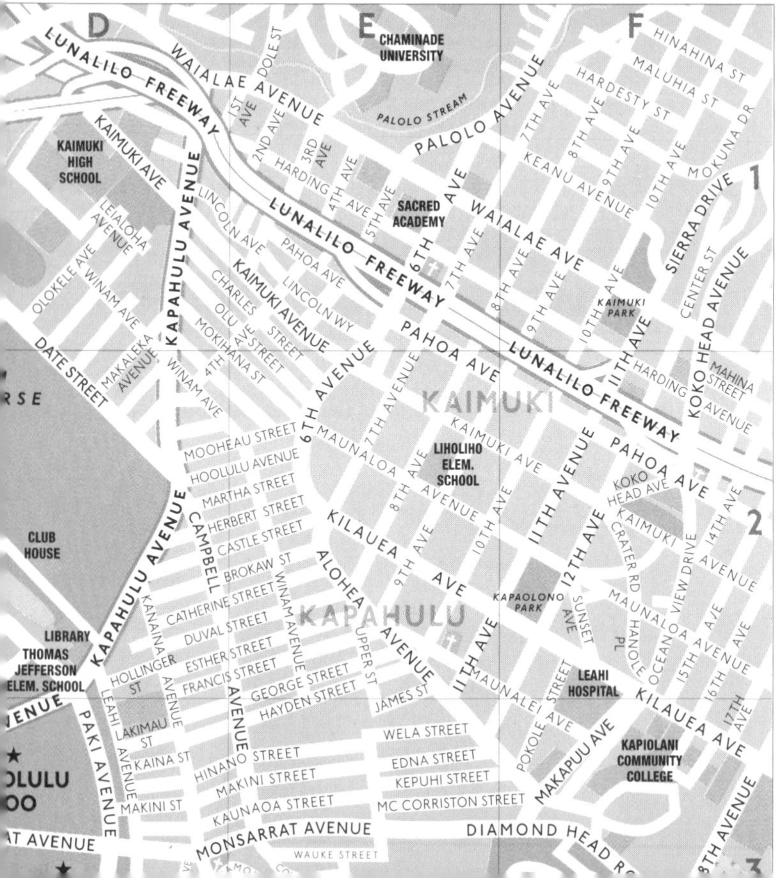

D
E
F
1
2
3
CHAMINADE UNIVERSITY
KAIMUKI HIGH SCHOOL
SACRED ACADEMY
KAIMUKI PARK
KAIMUKI
LIHOLIHO ELEM. SCHOOL
CLUB HOUSE
KAPAOLONO PARK
KAPAHULU
LIBRARY
THOMAS JEFFERSON ELEM. SCHOOL
LEAHI HOSPITAL
KAPIOLANI COMMUNITY COLLEGE
LUNALILO FREEWAY
WAIALAE AVENUE
WAIALAE AVE
PALOLO AVENUE
PALOLO STREAM
DOLE ST
1ST AVE
2ND AVE
3RD AVE
4TH AVE
5TH AVE
6TH AVE
6TH AVENUE
7TH AVE
7TH AVENUE
8TH AVE
9TH AVE
10TH AVE
11TH AVE
11TH AVENUE
12TH AVE
14TH AVE
15TH AVE
16TH AVE
17TH AVE
8TH AVENUE
HINAHINA ST
MALUHIA ST
HARDESTY ST
MOKUNA DR
KEANU AVENUE
SIERRA DRIVE
CENTER ST
KOKO HEAD AVENUE
KOKO HEAD AVE
MAHINA STREET
HARDING
HARDING AVE
KAIMUKI AVE
KAIMUKI AVENUE
LINCOLN AVE
LINCOLN WY
PAHOA AVE
CHARLES STREET
OLU STREET
4TH AVE
MOKIHANA ST
WINAM AVE
LEIALOHA AVENUE
OLOKELE AVE
MAKALEKA AVENUE
DATE STREET
KAPAHULU AVENUE
MOOHEAU STREET
HOOLULU AVENUE
MARTHA STREET
HERBERT STREET
CASTLE STREET
BROKAW ST
CATHERINE STREET
DUVAL STREET
ESTHER STREET
FRANCIS STREET
GEORGE STREET
HAYDEN STREET
CAMPBELL AVENUE
WINAM AVENUE
KANAINA AVENUE
HOLLINGER ST
LEAHI AVENUE
LAKIMAU ST
KAINA ST
MAKINI ST
PAKI AVENUE
UPPER ST
JAMES ST
ALOHEA AVENUE
KILAUEA AVE
MAUNALOA AVENUE
MAUNALEI AVE
POKOLE STREET
SUNSET AVE
CRATER RD
KAIMUKI
VIEW DRIVE
OCEAN
HANOLE PL
MAKAPUU AVE
WELA STREET
EDNA STREET
KEPUHI STREET
MC CORRISTON STREET
HINANO STREET
MAKINI STREET
KAUNAOA STREET
MONSARRAT AVENUE
WAUKE STREET
DIAMOND HEAD RD

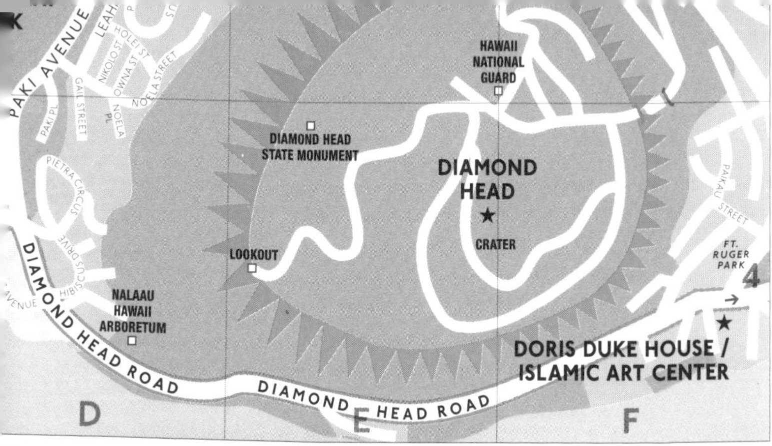
PAKI AVENUE
LEAHI
HOLEI ST
NIKOLO ST
OWNA ST
NOELA STREET
GAIL STREET
PAKI PL
NOELA PL
PIETRA CIRCUS
HIBISCUS DRIVE
DIAMOND HEAD ROAD
HAWAII NATIONAL GUARD
DIAMOND HEAD STATE MONUMENT
DIAMOND HEAD
CRATER
LOOKOUT
NALAAU HAWAII ARBORETUM
PAIKAU STREET
FT. RUGER PARK
4
DORIS DUKE HOUSE / ISLAMIC ART CENTER
DIAMOND HEAD ROAD
D
E
F

PUNAHOU SCHOOL WALL

MAGIC ISLAND BEACH

ɜdium-sized outdoor ›hitheater, the Waikiki l is one of Hawaii's concert venues. ɹ can, try to attend a aiian music concert ›er the stars (the Shell · hosts jazz and rock). The Shell, which is :her dull imitation of ney's Opera House, s have seats, but ›'re hard and omfortable; far better ring a picnic, sit on the ;s, and watch as your ;hbors – men and nen both – dance hula ıe songs. Adjoining ,olani Park is ctuated by graceful, shedding shower trees, and makes a good picnic or kite-flying spot on a lazy afternoon.

Honolulu Zoo (**A** D3)
→ *151 Kapahulu Ave*
Tel. 971-7171
Daily 9am–4.30pm
In a little pocket of green off Kapiolani Park sits Honolulu's charming zoo. There's all the expected animals of any mid-size city zoo – giraffes, monkeys, camels – but it's also home to some massive, slow-moving Galápagos turtles (among other forms of rare and endangered sea turtles) and an expanded collection of various birds, including the nene goose, Hawaii's state bird.
Best of all, the zoo also hosts monthly live music (mostly Hawaiian or jazz); pick up a platter of takeout sushi and watch the sun set over Diamond Head.

Diamond Head (**A** E4)
→ *Take Monsarrat Ave to Diamond Head Rd*
Diamond Head – so named for its profile, which looks like a giant, roughly faceted diamond – is a now-extinct volcano and possibly Oahu's most famous natural formation. The hike to the crater itself is fairly dull (and awfully steep), but probably won't take you much more than a half hour, and it's worth it for the sweeping vistas it affords of the island's entire south coast.

Punahou School Wall
(off map, north of **A**)
→ *1601 Punahou St (toward Manoa)*
This 160-year-old private school is bordered by a low, porous lava-stone wall banked with crawling tentacles of night-blooming cereus. In late summer and early spring, the plant, whose flowers bloom only at night, bursts into ghostly, intoxicating blooms. Stop here one evening for a picture or just to inhale.

KAWAIHAO CHURCH CEMETERY

FOSTER BOTANICAL GARDEN

FEDERAL BUILDING
CHANNEL ST
SOUTH ST
KEAWE S
QUEEN
PLEASTON AVENUE
BUFORD AVENUE
FORT AMSTRONG
FORREST AVENUE
AUAHI STREET
KEAWE STREET
CORAL STREET
LANA LN
COOKE ST
HALEKAU
5
ILALO STREET
CORAL STREET
LANA LN
COOKE STREET
OHE STREET
KOULA ST
AUAHI STRE
KAKAAKO
KELIKOI STREET
ILALO ST
ST
OHE STREET
KOULA
AHUI STREET
KAKAAKO WATERFRONT PARK
OLOMEHANI ST
KEWAL BASIN
6
MAMALA BAY
A
B

King Kamehameha Statue (**B** B3)
Across the street from Iolani Palace stands a large bronze statue of King Kamehameha the Great, who unified the eight islands in 1795. On May Day, which commemorates the king's triumph, the statue is heaped with ropes of flower leis.

Iolani Palace (**B** B3)
→ *Corner of King and Richard Sts Tel. 538-1471 Tue-Sat 9am–2.15pm; 45-min guided tours every 15 mins*
Completed by King David Kalakaua in 1882, this lava-stone and wood palace later became a prison for Hawaii's last monarch, Queen Liliuokalani, who was kept under house arrest after her overthrow in 1893. The only royal palace in America has been beautifully restored, with gleaming wood floors and swags of Scalamandre silk.

The Honolulu Academy of Arts (**B** D4)
→ *900 South Beretania St Tel. 532-8700 Tue-Sat 10am–4.30pm (5pm Sun)*
Founded by the descendants of prominent missionary families, the academy is now home to an impressive collection of Asian and Western art, including a splendid mix of native Pacific arts and crafts and the late James Michener's renowned ukiyo-e collection. The café is excellent and the annex, the Linekona School, hosts shows by local artists.

Mission Houses Museum (**B** B4)
→ *553 South King St Tel. 531-0481 Tue-Sat 9am–4pm*
Some of the Hawaiian Islands' earliest Western visitors were Christian missionaries, who sailed from New England in the early 19th century. A small clutch of the missionaries' tidy whitewashed wood houses occupies a modest green oasis in downtow Honolulu. Nearby, on P bowl Street, is Kawaiha Church, built around 18 and the island's oldest church. The beloved Ka hameha V is entombed small mausoleum on th church's grounds.

Foster Botanical Garden (**B** B1)
→ *50 North Vineyard Bl Tel. 533-6335 Daily 9am–*
Here is every tropical pl imaginable, rare specim of both imported and indigenous plant life. Especially impressive a some of the palm trees, which look positively prehistoric.

KING KAMEHAMEHA

IOLANI PALACE

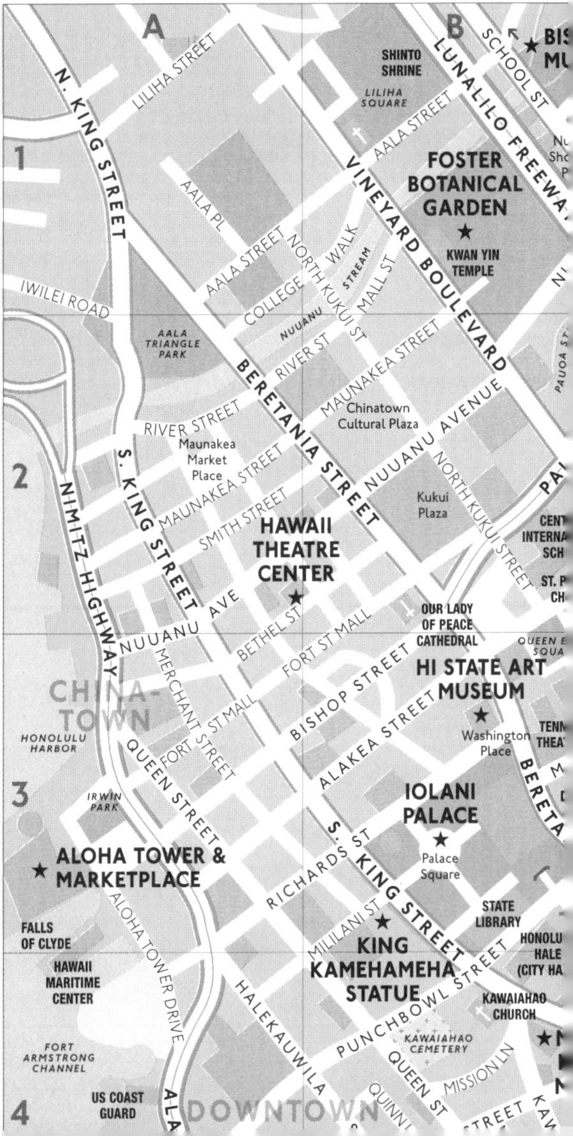
A
B
1
2
3
4
N. KING STREET
LILIHA STREET
SHINTO SHRINE
LILIHA SQUARE
AALA STREET
SCHOOL ST
LUNALILO FREEWAY
FOSTER BOTANICAL GARDEN
KWAN YIN TEMPLE
VINEYARD BOULEVARD
AALA PL
NORTH KUKUI ST
WALK
STREAM
MALL ST
COLLEGE
NUUANU
IWILEI ROAD
AALA TRIANGLE PARK
BERETANIA STREET
RIVER ST
MAUNAKEA STREET
Chinatown Cultural Plaza
NUUANU AVENUE
PAUOA ST
RIVER STREET
Maunakea Market Place
SMITH STREET
NORTH KUKUI STREET
Kukui Plaza
HAWAII THEATRE CENTER
S. KING STREET
NIMITZ HIGHWAY
NUUANU AVE
BETHEL ST
FORT ST MALL
MERCHANT STREET
OUR LADY OF PEACE CATHEDRAL
CHINA-TOWN
HONOLULU HARBOR
BISHOP STREET
HI STATE ART MUSEUM
Washington Place
QUEEN STREET
ALAKEA STREET
IOLANI PALACE
Palace Square
IRWIN PARK
ALOHA TOWER & MARKETPLACE
RICHARDS ST
KING STREET
STATE LIBRARY
HONOLULU HALE (CITY HA
MILILANI ST
KING KAMEHAMEHA STATUE
FALLS OF CLYDE
HAWAII MARITIME CENTER
ALOHA TOWER DRIVE
HALEKAUWILA
PUNCHBOWL STREET
KAWAIAHAO CHURCH
KAWAIAHAO CEMETERY
FORT ARMSTRONG CHANNEL
US COAST GUARD
DOWNTOWN
QUEEN ST
MISSION LN
QUINN

Just west of Waikiki's cheerfully seedy hustle are the neighborhoods of old Honolulu – Chinatown, Downtown, Kakaako and Nuuanu. The buildings of these neighborhoods, from Kawaihao Church in Downtown to the narrow dusty storefronts of Chinatown, evoke the brief period in 19th-century Honolulu when native Hawaiian royalty, enterprising American businessmen and Christian missionaries coexisted in a society both fractious and transformative. The area also boasts some of the islands' most treasured landmarks, notably Iolani Palace. And just a few blocks away is the marvelously scented Maunakea Street, flanked by a half dozen lei shops.

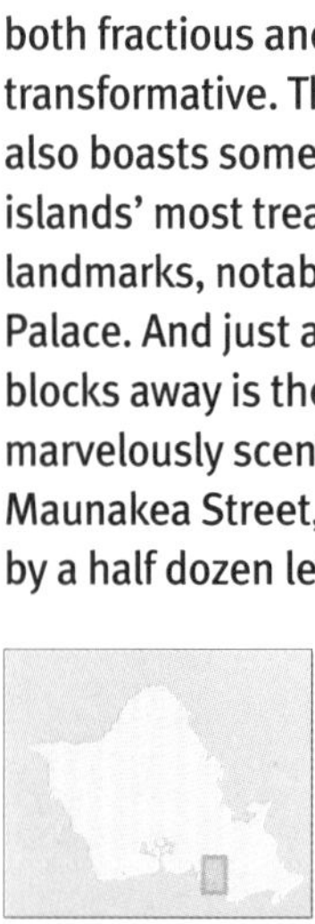

SHUNG CHONG YUEIN LTD

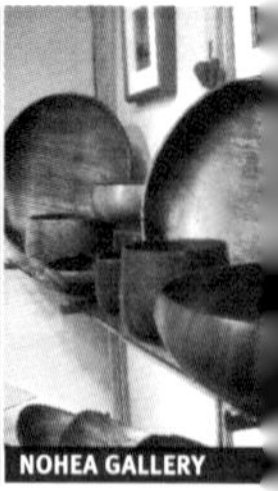

NOHEA GALLERY

RESTAURANTS

Pho Bac (**B** B1)
→ *901 River St*
Tel. 528-4097
Daily 8am–7.30pm
Pho – the delicately seasoned Vietnamese beef soup – is the only thing on the menu at this modest, inexpensive restaurant, but one sip of the light, lemony broth will make you understand the queue that forms outside every day.
À la carte $6.

Duc's Bistro (**B** A2)
→ *1188 Maunakea St*
Tel. 531-6325
Daily 11.30am–1.30pm; 5.30–10pm (closed Sat-Sun lunch)
Before French-Vietnamese cuisine was trendy, this quiet and intimate spot served food so inventive, it soon became a local favorite. The seafood – especially the tarragon prawns – is always excellent, as is the duck. Good for a romantic dinner or lazy evening meal, especially when the live jazz band's playing.
À la carte $19.

A Little Bit of Saigon (**B** A2)
→ *1160 Maunakea St*
Tel. 528-3663
Daily 10am–10pm
At lunchtime, aloha shirt-clad lawyers and businessmen crowd this Vietnamese restaurant for its flavorful *pho* and delicate spring rolls. At night, a more eclectic crowd appears, from couples and families to young locals readying themselves for a bit of bar-hopping. À la carte $12.

BARS, NIGHTLIFE

Indigo (**B** A2)
→ *1121 Nuuanu Ave*
Tel. 521-2900 Tue-Fri 11.30am–2pm; Tue-Sat 6pm–varies (often depends on Hawaii Theatre's event)
The real draw of this Pan-Asian spot is its casual colonial decor and its garden, which is lit at night by dozens of twinkling lights and swinging hurricane lamps. After dark, the bar area becomes a moody, atmospheric lounge. Reservations advised. À la carte $19.

Side Street Inn (**B** D5)
→ *1225 Hopaka St*
Tel. 591-0253
Mon-Fri 10.30am–1pm; Pupus: daily 4pm–1am; Bar: daily 2pm–2am
After the last meal's been served, virtually every big-name chef in Honolulu (including Roy Yamaguchi

CHINATOWN MARKET

RAKU
2003
Exhibition

THE ARTS AT MARK'S GARAGE

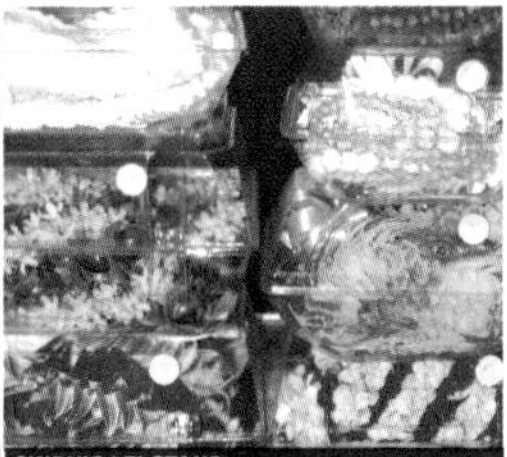

CINDY'S LEI STAND

and Alan Wong) decamps to this hole-in-the-wall – one of Hawaii's few late-night joints – for saimin, ribs and fried rice, not to mention as much alcohol as they can quaff.

SHOPPING

Native Books Na Mea Hawaii (**B** C6)
→ *At Ward Warehouse, 1050 Ala Moana Blvd*
Tel. 596-8885 Mon-Sat 10am–9pm (5pm Sun)
This unique co-op sells work by native Hawaiian artisans, including museum-quality – and pricey – Ni'ihau shell necklaces, carved gourds, feather leis, and lathe-turned native hardwood bowls; also a good selection of books in Hawaiian and English.

Nohea Gallery (**B** C6)
→ *At Ward Warehouse 1050 Ala Moana Blvd*
Tel. 596-0074 Mon-Sat 10am–9pm (5pm Sun) (plus two other branches)
This 12-year old, family-owned gallery offers the island's most extensive collection of work by local artists, from paintings to woven-gold bracelets and rings, but it's best known for its lathe-turned native hardwood bowls.

Cindy's Lei Stand
Lin's Lei Stand (**B** A2)
→ *1034 Maunakea St*
Tel. 536-2169
Daily 6am–9pm
→ *1017 Maunakea St*
Tel. 537-4112
Daily 6.45am–10pm
Maunakea Street is dotted with lei stands, but Lin's and Cindy's have the island favorites, including the delicate green pakalana blossoms and the trumpet-shaped, heavenly puakenikeni flowers. Both can provide pricier, special order flowers (like the pale purple crown flower) and both ship leis, wrapped in fresh ti leaves, to the Mainland.

The ARTS at Mark's Garage (**B** A2)
→ *1159 Nuuanu Ave*
Tel. 521-2923
Tue-Sat 11am–6pm
By day a gallery, by night a performance space, this vibrant young artists' co-operative is an eclectic introduction to the island's contemporary arts scene. Most of the work (usually quite affordable) is for sale, and the staff is friendly and approachable.

Salon .5 (**B** A2)
→ *1160 Nuuanu Ave*
Tel. 550-2855 Call ahead as opening times vary
Catty-corner from the ARTS at Mark's Garage is this small knuckle of a gallery, which sells paintings, drawings and etchings by up-and-coming local artists.

Robyn Buntin (**B** D4)
→ *848 and 820 South Beretania St*
Tel. 523-5913 and 545-5572
Mon-Sat 10am–5pm
The Asian half of these two side-by-side galleries (the other sells Oceanic art) is well known and highly regarded for their collection of Japanese netsuke and woodblock prints. The Pacifica gallery offers stacks of 18th-, 19th- and early-to-mid-20th-century etchings, lithographs and sketches of Hawaii and Polynesia, and stunning found art.

Shung Chong Yuein Ltd (**B** A2)
→ *1027 Maunakea St*
Tel. 531-1983 Mon-Sat 6am–5:30pm (2pm Sun)
You can buy almost any sort of sugared fruit or Chinese pastry from this quaint, steamy bakery and sweet shop, whose plate-glass windows and wooden cabinetry give it the air of an old-time apothecary's. Gingered mango or coconut is sold by the pound, but don't leave without trying a flaky, fruity Chinese wedding cake.

Ming's (**B** A3)
→ *1144 Bethel St*
Tel. 585-8877
Tue-Sat 10am–4.30pm
Behind its modest, plate-glass façade, this dusty, sleepy shoebox of a store is packed with a well-edited collection of Chinese antiquities, including cinnabar-red armoires, low benches made out of soft, lustrous wood, and delicate teacups and pastry molds. Its owner, who is usually on-site, is as friendly and gracious as he is knowledgeable.

Chinatown Farmers' Market (**B** A2)
→ *At Chinatown Cultural Plaza, Maunakea and Beretania Sts*
Every tropical or Asian fish, fruit, flower, vegetable or spice you could ever want is in these buzzing, colorful indoor and outdoor markets where vendors have everything from purple basil to honeycomb tripe to pig's feet and orchids. An enthusiastic and aggressive crowd of chefs, Chinese grand-mothers, young couples and ladies-who-lunch shop here.

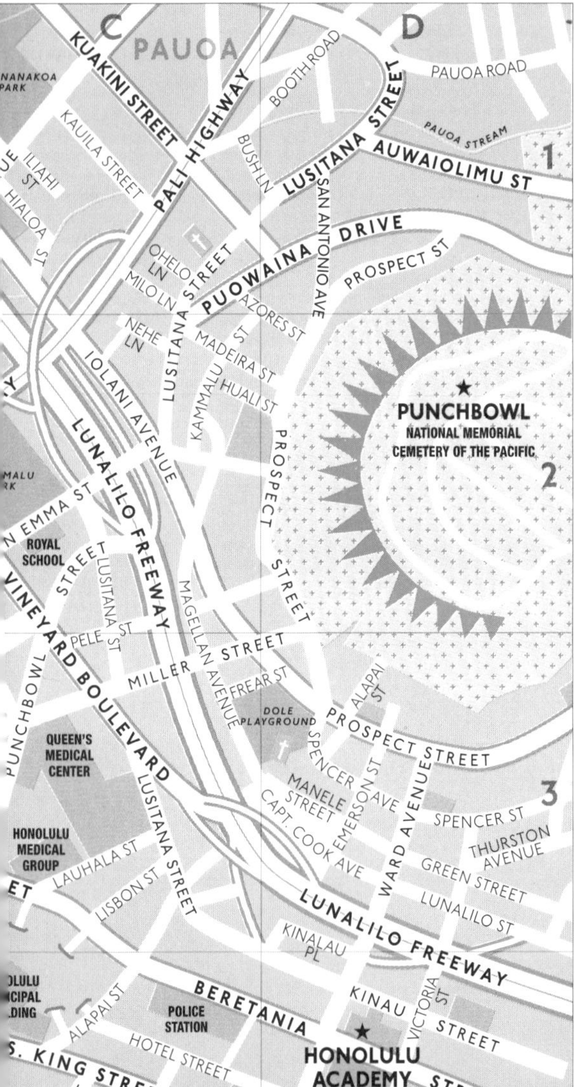
C
D
PAUOA
NANAKOA PARK
KUAKINI STREET
PALI HIGHWAY
BOOTH ROAD
PAUOA ROAD
LUSITANA STREET
PAUOA STREAM
KAUILA STREET
BUSH LN
AUWAIOLIMU ST
ILIAHI ST
HIALOA ST
SAN ANTONIO AVE
PUOWAINA DRIVE
PROSPECT ST
OHELO LN
MILO LN
AZORES ST
NEHE LN
MADEIRA ST
HUALI ST
KAMMALU ST
IOLANI AVENUE
PUNCHBOWL
NATIONAL MEMORIAL
CEMETERY OF THE PACIFIC
LUNALILO FREEWAY
PROSPECT STREET
N EMMA ST
ROYAL SCHOOL
VINEYARD BOULEVARD
LUSITANA ST
MAGELLAN AVENUE
PELE ST
MILLER STREET
FREAR ST
ALAPAI ST
DOLE PLAYGROUND
PUNCHBOWL
QUEEN'S MEDICAL CENTER
SPENCER AVE
MANELE STREET
EMERSON ST
WARD AVENUE
SPENCER ST
CAPT. COOK AVE
THURSTON AVENUE
HONOLULU MEDICAL GROUP
LAUHALA ST
LISBON ST
GREEN STREET
LUNALILO ST
KINALAU PL
BERETANIA
KINAU STREET
VICTORIA ST
POLICE STATION
HOTEL STREET
S. KING STREET
HONOLULU ACADEMY OF ARTS
STRAUB CLINIC
1
2
3
4

BISHOP MUSEUM

STATE ART MUSEUM

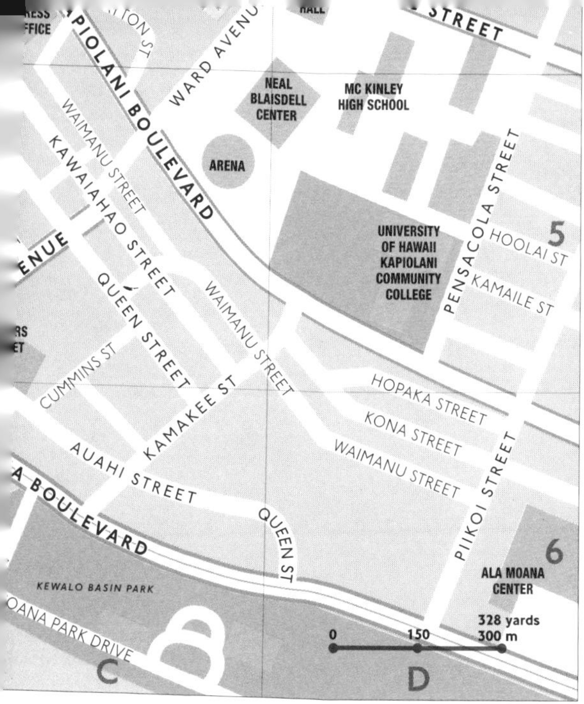
STREET
KAPIOLANI BOULEVARD
WARD AVENUE
NEAL BLAISDELL CENTER
MC KINLEY HIGH SCHOOL
ARENA
WAIMANU STREET
KAWAIAHAO STREET
UNIVERSITY OF HAWAII KAPIOLANI COMMUNITY COLLEGE
PENSACOLA STREET
HOOLAI ST
KAMAILE ST
5
QUEEN STREET
WAIMANU STREET
CUMMINS ST
KAMAKEE ST
HOPAKA STREET
KONA STREET
WAIMANU STREET
PIIKOI STREET
AUAHI STREET
BOULEVARD
QUEEN ST
6
ALA MOANA CENTER
KEWALO BASIN PARK
0
150
328 yards
300 m
C
D

PUNCHBOWL

HAWAII THEATRE CENTER

vaii Theatre ter (**B** A2)
130 Bethel St 528-0506 Hours vary, ahead; tours on 1st and Tue of month
breathtaking rococo-ets-Art Deco theater built in 1922 and gnificently restored ears later. Today, the ater hosts Honolulu's and film festivals, as as any number of ing (and local) dance theater troupes.

te Art Museum (**B** B3)
Jo 1 Capitol District Bldg, South Hotel St, Floor Tel. 586-0900 Sat 10am–4pm
This relatively new museum displays some of the best work by Hawaii artists acquired by the State Foundation on Culture and the Arts. The mix, while wildly eclectic, is still a fascinating introduction to the island's art scene. The museum's beautiful quarters was built during the reign of Kamehameha V.

Aloha Tower Marketplace (**B** A3)
→ 1 Aloha Tower Drive, Suite 3000 Tel. 528-5700
Twentysomethings and visiting expats flock here to the clutch of bars and restaurants, especially the microbrewery Gordon Biersch, which has a spectacular view of Honolulu Harbor. The marketplace is worth a visit when it hosts a Hawaiian music festival or concert. Also, naval fans might like to watch the *Independence* and *Constitution* set sail, which they do around 9 or 10pm Saturday evening.

Punchbowl (**B** D2) **National Memorial Cemetery of the Pacific**
→ 2177 Puowaina Drive Daily 8.30am–5.30pm (6.30pm March-Sep)
This crisply maintained cemetery contains the graves of 25,000 servicemen who fought in World War II, the Korean War and in Vietnam. It can be a sobering experience, but there are fabulous views of Waikiki.

Bishop Museum (**B** north of B1)
→ 1525 Bernice St Tel. 847-3511 Daily 9am–5pm
This distinguished stone museum houses the most extensive and valuable collection of Hawaiiana and ancient artifacts in the world, from tapa cloth made of pounded bark to hand-hewn outrigger canoes and, most impressively, many artifacts from the royal family. Note: most of the museum is not air conditioned and should be saved for cool days.

LOBSTER CLAW AT THE LYON ARBORETUM

CONTEMPORARY MUSEUM

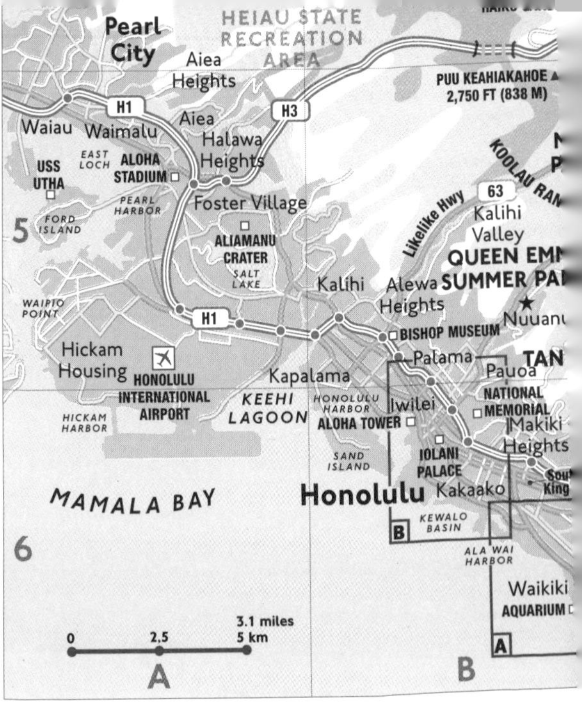
Pearl City
HEIAU STATE RECREATION AREA
Aiea Heights
PUU KEAHIAKAHOE
2,750 FT (838 M)
H1
H3
Waiau
Waimalu
Aiea
Halawa Heights
USS UTHA
EAST LOCH
ALOHA STADIUM
PEARL HARBOR
Foster Village
KOOLAU RAN
63
Likelike Hwy
Kalihi Valley
5
FORD ISLAND
ALIAMANU CRATER
SALT LAKE
QUEEN EM
SUMMER PA
Kalihi
Alewa Heights
WAIPIO POINT
BISHOP MUSEUM
Nuuan
Palama
TAN
Hickam Housing
HONOLULU INTERNATIONAL AIRPORT
Kapalama
Pauoa
NATIONAL MEMORIAL
KEEHI LAGOON
HONOLULU HARBOR
Iwilei
HICKAM HARBOR
ALOHA TOWER
Makiki Heights
SAND ISLAND
IOLANI PALACE
MAMALA BAY
Honolulu
Kakaako
KEWALO BASIN
B
6
ALA WAI HARBOR
Waikiki
AQUARIUM
0
2.5
3.1 miles
5 km
A
A
B

Hanauma Bay (**C** D6)
One of the world's most renowned snorkeling spots, this bay's dark-blue waters are full of exotic fish, as bold as their colors, who rarely dart away from swimmers. The successful push to save the coral reef means no feeding the fish.

Chinese Cemetery (**C** C6)
One of the most beautiful spots in Manoa is the Chinese Cemetery, deep in the valley on a gently sloping hill with fabulous views. One of the oldest cemeteries (Chang Apana, the real-life Charlie Chan, is buried here), it attracts multi-generational local families coming to pay their respects, who leave behind offerings of food or flowers.

Lyon Arboretum / Manoa Falls (**C** C5)
→ *3860 Manoa Rd*
Tel. 988-0456
These breathtaking gardens are well worth the mud and clouds of mosquitoes. If you're feeling more adventurous, the hike up to Manoa Falls is aerobic but otherwise easy – and you're rewarded with a fantastic, roaring waterfall.

The Contemporary Museum (**C** B6)
→ *2411 Makiki Heights Drive*
Tel. 526-1322 Tue-Sat 10am–4pm; Sun noon–4pm
This gorgeous little museum, once a private residence, contains eclectic, often surprising works. The permanent exhibit, David Hockney's set for the operetta *L'Enfant et les Sortileges*, and the wondrously landscaped garden are also a big draw.

Queen Emma's Summer Palace (**C** B5)
→ *2913 Pali Hwy*
Tel. 595-3167 Daily 9am–4pm
Queen Emma, who married King Kamehameha IV in 1856, was one of Hawaii's most beloved royals. She retreated to this small palace in cool, shady Nuuanu Valley to escape the heat of Honolulu. Mode but lovely, it is filled wit memorabilia from Quee Victoria and of her only the beloved Prince Albe who died, like many members of the Hawaii royal family, at a very yo age.

Tantalus (**C** B6)
One of Honolulu's most famous mountain range Tantalus offers some amazing views of the ci from its many lookout points. Roll down your windows while driving u the twisty road: the air i sweet and fresh with th delicate scent of wild w and yellow ginger.

HANAUMA BAY

CHINESE CEMETERY

QUEEN EMMA'S SUMMER PALACE

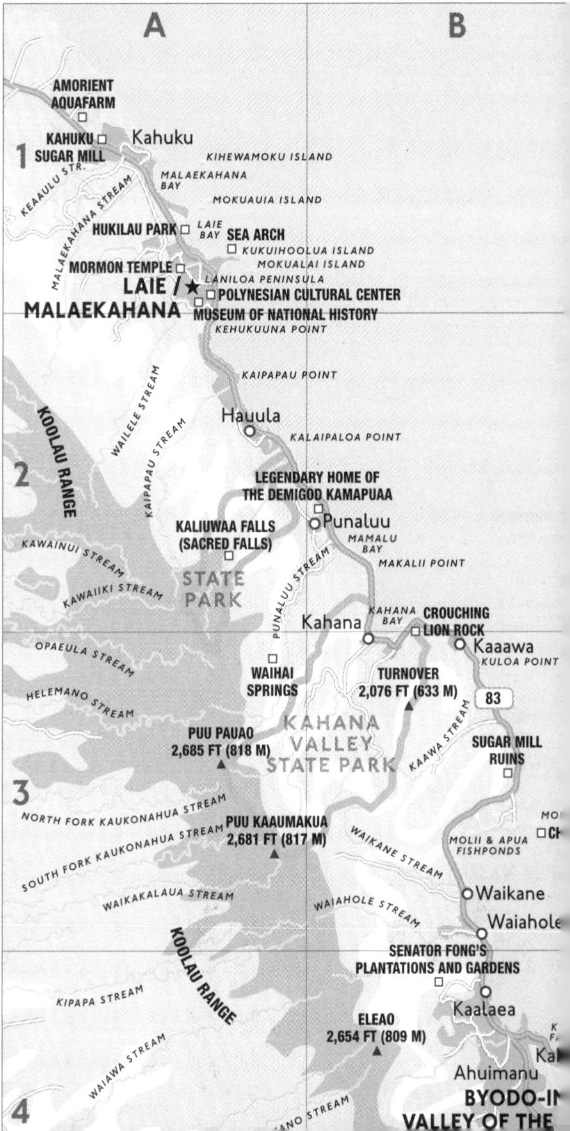

A
B
1
2
3
4
AMORIENT AQUAFARM
KAHUKU SUGAR MILL
Kahuku
KIHEWAMOKU ISLAND
KEAAULU STR.
MALAEKAHANA BAY
MALAEKAHANA STREAM
MOKUAUIA ISLAND
HUKILAU PARK
LAIE BAY
SEA ARCH
KUKUIHOOLUA ISLAND
MOKUALAI ISLAND
MORMON TEMPLE
LANILOA PENINSULA
LAIE / MALAEKAHANA
POLYNESIAN CULTURAL CENTER
MUSEUM OF NATIONAL HISTORY
KEHUKUUNA POINT
KAIPAPAU POINT
WAILELE STREAM
KOOLAU RANGE
KAIPAPAU STREAM
Hauula
KALAIPALOA POINT
LEGENDARY HOME OF THE DEMIGOD KAMAPUAA
Punaluu
KALIUWAA FALLS (SACRED FALLS)
MAMALU BAY
KAWAINUI STREAM
MAKALII POINT
STATE PARK
KAWAIIKI STREAM
PUNALUU STREAM
Kahana
KAHANA BAY
CROUCHING LION ROCK
Kaaawa
KULOA POINT
OPAEULA STREAM
WAIHAI SPRINGS
TURNOVER 2,076 FT (633 M)
83
HELEMANO STREAM
PUU PAUAO 2,685 FT (818 M)
KAHANA VALLEY STATE PARK
KAAWA STREAM
SUGAR MILL RUINS
NORTH FORK KAUKONAHUA STREAM
PUU KAAUMAKUA 2,681 FT (817 M)
SOUTH FORK KAUKONAHUA STREAM
WAIKANE STREAM
MOLII & APUA FISHPONDS
Waikane
WAIKAKALAUA STREAM
WAIAHOLE STREAM
Waiahole
KOOLAU RANGE
SENATOR FONG'S PLANTATIONS AND GARDENS
KIPAPA STREAM
Kaalaea
ELEAO 2,654 FT (809 M)
WAIAWA STREAM
Ahuimanu

Honolulu is a small town, but few tourists venture into two of Hawaii's most beautiful residential neighborhoods, Manoa and Tantalus. This is a shame, because aside from boasting some of the city's best restaurants, a trip into the valley or up the mountain is a fascinating architectural tour. The easy trip back to Waikiki will take you past the University of Hawaii, which hosts interesting concerts and shows. Not many visitors stray to the Windward side of Oahu either, home to two of the island's largest suburban towns, Kailua and Kaneohe. But this part of the island is also notable for its clean beaches, lush foliage and dramatic green cliffs.

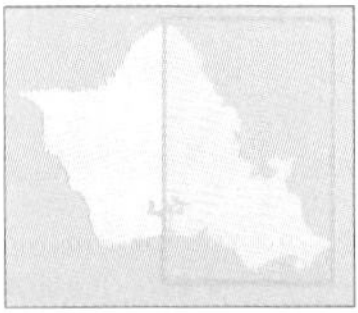

chef mavro
CHEF MAVRO

HILDGUND JEWELERS

RESTAURANTS

Andy's Sandwiches (**C** C6)
→ *2904 East Manoa Rd, Manoa Valley*
Tel. 988-6161 Daily 7.30am–5pm (4pm Fri)
This Manoa mainstay makes the valley's freshest and tastiest health-food sandwiches and salads: the turkey sandwiches are made with fresh shredded meat, and heaped with thick wedges of just-picked avocado. The staff, including owner Andy, who's usually behind the counter, are among the nicest you'll encounter. Around $3.50 for a sandwich.

Zippy's (**C** B6)
→ *1765 South King St*
Tel. 453-3715
Daily 24 hrs
Hawaii's most popular chain diner serves fresh-market fish, saimin, chili, and teriyaki burgers (along with just about anything else you can imagine). Its best dish – a rich, meaty oxtail soup – is a complex blend of cilantro, peanuts, grated ginger and, of course, thick chunks of fatty, flavorful meat. À la carte $5–$14.

Island Manapua (**C** C6)
→ *Manoa Marketplace, Manoa Valley Tel. 988-5441 Mon-Fri 7.30am–7pm (5pm Sat); Sun 8.30am–5pm*
A local favorite, this take-away joint serves some of the best fast-food Chinese on the island, from doughy chow fun noodles topped with shredded *char siu*, to bittermelon and tofu. The plate lunches – two entrées and one starch – are enormous and make a perfect picnic for two. Plate lunch around $6.

Sushi Sasabune (**C** B6)
→ *1419 South King St*
Tel. 947-3800
Mon-Fri noon–2pm; Mon-Sat 5.30–10pm
Forgive the dark, dreary interior and sit down at the bar for some of the best sushi you'll have anywhere. Picky eaters beware: the bar is strictly *omakase* – chef's choice. But don't worry, Sasabune's sushi is made with warm rice and perfectly cut pieces of fresh Pacific fish, and everything you'll eat will be a wonder. À la carte $8.

Yamagen (**C** B6)
→ *2210 South King St*
Tel. 947-2125
Daily 5.30–9:30pm
Almost inconspicuous

F JAVA

ROY'S

ALAN WONG'S

amid the bustle of King Street, Yamagen looks more like a tarpaper-windowed shack in rural Meiji-era Japan than a restaurant. But request one of the four outdoor tables (it's always terribly hot and steamy inside), and you'll enjoy one of the best local Japanese meals in Honolulu, including thick, chewy *udon* and perfectly fried tempura. The staff is incredibly friendly. À la carte around $8.

Alan Wong's (**C** B6)
→ *1857 South King St Tel. 949-1758 Daily from 5pm (last seating is at 9pm)*
Arguably the best Pacific Rim restaurant in Hawaii, Alan Wong's eponymous restaurant turns out terrifically accomplished and confident Asian-inspired cuisine in which humble local favorites are given a posh and inventive spin. Particularly fine are the rare-seared *ahi* and *opihi* shooter appetizers and the ginger-crusted *opakapaka* entrée; the wine list is equally sunny and fresh. Reservations required. À la carte $25.

Roy's (**C** D6)
→ *6700 Kalanianaole Hwy Tel. 396-7697 Mon-Thu 5.30–9.30pm (10pm Fri; 9pm Sat); Sun 5–9.30pm*
One of the most famous – and established – restaurants specializing in high-end Pacific Rim cuisine, Roy's is known for its meltingly fresh fish, savory meat dishes, and friendly service. Chef Roy Yamaguchi now owns some two dozen satellites of his eponymous restaurant; this one was his first. À la carte about $26.

Chef Mavro (**C** B6)
→ *1969 South King St Tel. 944-4714 Tue-Sun 6–9:30pm*
French haute cuisine meets the Pacific Rim jollity at Chef Mavro, one of Honolulu's most popular and highly acclaimed high-end restaurants. Foodies the world over love its inventive combinations and emphasis on fresh cuisine, as do locals, who pack it full every night. À la carte $27.

ICE CREAM PARLOR

Waiola Shave Ice (**C** B6)
→ *2135 Waiola St Tel. 949-2269 Daily 7.30am–6.30pm*
Shave ice – a paper cone or cup packed with finely ground ice saturated with flavored sugar syrup – is a favorite post-beach (or pre-beach, or post-meal) snack, and Waiola is an island favorite. Try it with a scoop of ice cream at the bottom, or topped with subtly sweet azuki beans. About $2.25.

SHOPPING

Hildgund Jewelers (**C** C6)
→ *In the shopping arcade of the Kahala Mandarin Oriental, 5000 Kahala Ave Tel. 737-8663 Daily 9am–9pm*
A local favorite and a Hawaii institution, the elegant and sophisticated Hildgund (which also maintains satellites on Maui and the Big Island) sells fantastic jeweled confections that have been made in Ida Oberstein, Germany, exclusively for its stores. The shop is particularly good with colored gems, many of which glint from whimsical brooches and sparkling rings and pendants. Hildgund also carries its own Hawaiian heirloom jewelry, and is in the process of re-creating a line of royal jewelry featuring the Hawaiian coat of arms.

Yama's Fish Market (**C** B6)
→ *2332 Young St, Manoa Valley Tel. 941-9994 Mon-Sat 9am–7pm (5pm Sun)*
Locals hankering for Hawaiian food drop by Yama's, which sells *kalua* pig, butterfish *laulau*, *huli-huli* (rotisserie) chicken, and *lomilomi* salmon by the pound. You can also buy plate lunches or snacks here, and the store can pack you a carry-on box of vacuum-sealed goodies so you can enjoy Hawaiian food at home.

East of Java (**C** B6)
Manoa Marketplace, Manoa Valley Tel. 988-5282 Mon-Sat 10am–6pm (2pm Sun)
Tinkling, dewy music wafts through this exotic, mellow store full of Indonesian furniture, crafts and handbags. Best of all, there's something for every price range, from a heavy, faintly scented bed to a small woven tube of incense to the enchanting insect-shaped kites hanging from the ceiling.

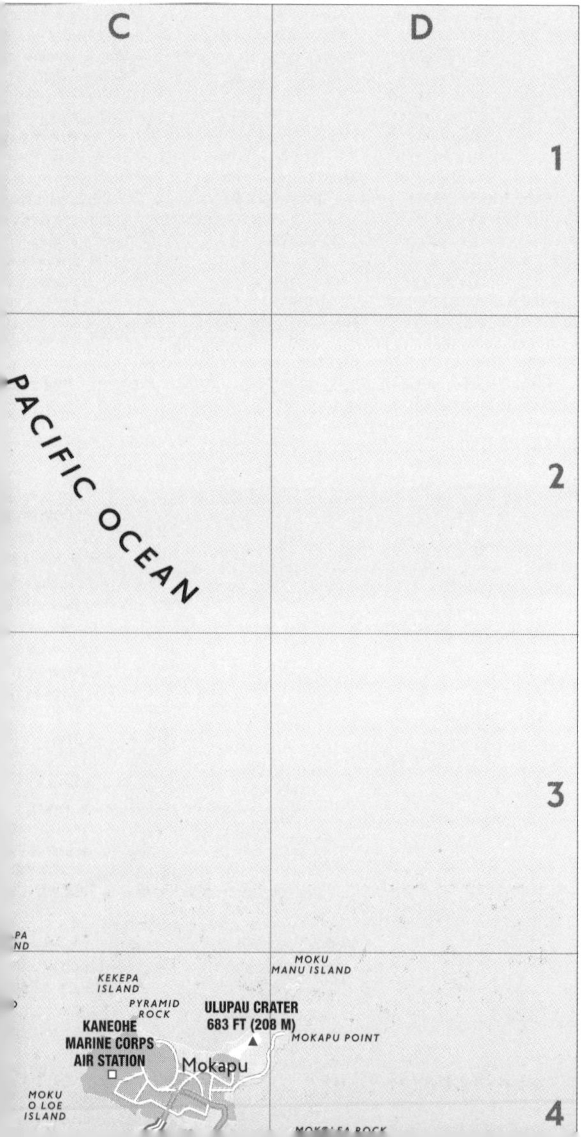
C
D
1
2
3
4
PACIFIC OCEAN
PA
ND
MOKU
MANU ISLAND
KEKEPA
ISLAND
PYRAMID
ROCK
ULUPAU CRATER
683 FT (208 M)
KANEOHE
MARINE CORPS
AIR STATION
MOKAPU POINT
Mokapu
MOKU
O LOE
ISLAND

NUUANU PALI LOOKOUT

LANIKAI BEACH

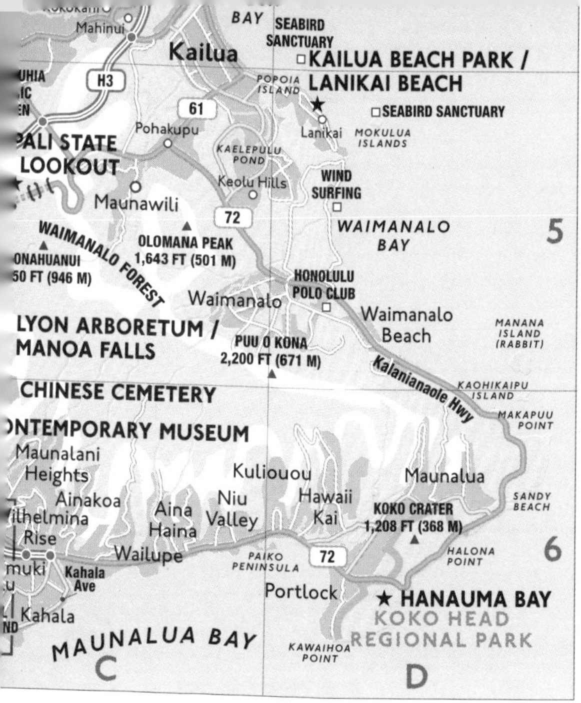

Mahinui
BAY
SEABIRD SANCTUARY
Kailua
KAILUA BEACH PARK / LANIKAI BEACH
H3
POPOIA ISLAND
61
SEABIRD SANCTUARY
Pohakupu
Lanikai
MOKULUA ISLANDS
PALI STATE LOOKOUT
KAELEPULU POND
Keolu Hills
WIND SURFING
Maunawili
72
WAIMANALO BAY
5
WAIMANALO FOREST
OLOMANA PEAK 1,643 FT (501 M)
HONOLULU POLO CLUB
Waimanalo
Waimanalo Beach
MANANA ISLAND (RABBIT)
LYON ARBORETUM / MANOA FALLS
PUU O KONA 2,200 FT (671 M)
Kalanianaole Hwy
KAOHIKAIPU ISLAND
CHINESE CEMETERY
MAKAPUU POINT
CONTEMPORARY MUSEUM
Maunalani Heights
Kuliouou
Maunalua
Ainakoa
Niu Valley
Hawaii Kai
SANDY BEACH
Wilhelmina Rise
Aina Haina
KOKO CRATER 1,208 FT (368 M)
Wailupe
PAIKO PENINSULA
72
HALONA POINT
6
Kahala Ave
Portlock
HANAUMA BAY
Kahala
KOKO HEAD REGIONAL PARK
MAUNALUA BAY
KAWAIHOA POINT
C
D

HONOLULU AND DIAMOND HEAD FROM TANTALUS

MALAEKAHANA

anu Pali State Park Lookout (C C5)
aily 4am–8pm
over a mile past Queen na's Summer Palace, park is remarkable for wesome lookout point, ch is where Kameha-a the Great unified the aiian islands in 1795 by ng the defeated Oahu riors over the sheer cliffs.

lua Beach Park / ikai Beach (C D5)
of Oahu's most popular beautiful beaches, they favorites of swimmers, akers, windsurfers, dlers and parasailers. can rent kayaks and le-person canoes near Kailua's parking lot, or just splash around in the pale (mostly calm) water. If you continue *mauka* down the beach, you'll eventually hit Lanikai, a jewel-like, short stretch of white sand flanked on one side by some of the area's most expensive real estate.

Byodo-in / Valley of the Temples (C B4)
→ 47-200 Kahekili Hwy
Tel. 239-8811
Daily 8am–4.30pm
The windward, lush, rainy side of the island is famous for its gardens and splendid greenery. In the interdenominational cemetery known as Valley of the Temples, chapels and monuments abound. The most popular is the candy-red Byodo-in, a replica of the famous 900-year-old Buddhist temple in Uji. Hawaii's version of the temple is beautiful but the dramatic mountains cupping it steal the show. A good reminder of what the Japanese have contributed to Hawaii, in culture and religion.

Laie and Malaekahana (C A1)
Continue north on Kamehameha Highway, and you'll drive through a quiet, tidy little town dotted with clapboard churches and shaggy ironwood pines. This is Laie, best known for its pervasive Mormon presence, including a satellite of the Mormon-run Brigham Young University. (The Mormon Church is also responsible for the Polynesian Cultural Center, a fascinating, though perhaps not in the way intended, South Pacific theme park that mixes genuinely interesting Polynesian performances with a good dose of squirm-inducing exploitation.) Laie is a beautiful stretch of land and it leads to Malaekahana Beach, a gorgeous, quiet expanse of sugary white sand gently lapped by clean, pale-blue water.

SHARK'S COVE

HAWAII'S PLANTATION VILLAGE

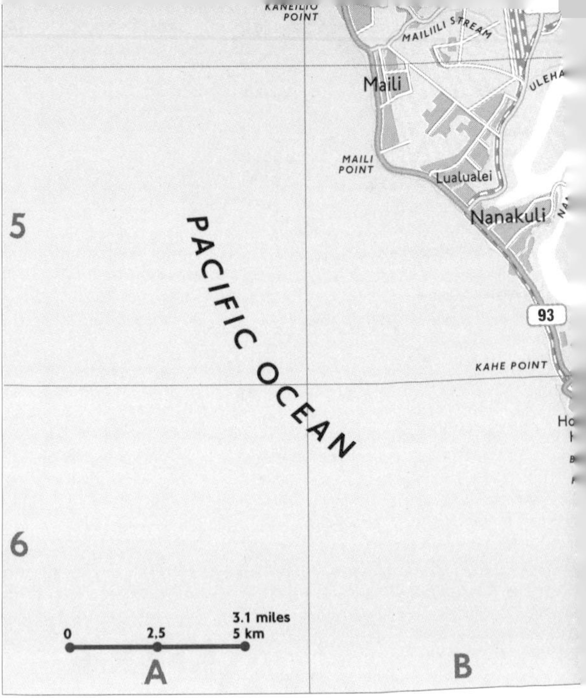
POINT
MAILIILI STREAM
Maili
MAILI POINT
Lualualei
Nanakuli
5
PACIFIC OCEAN
93
KAHE POINT
6
0
2,5
3.1 miles
5 km
A
B

Dole Plantation (**D** C3)
→ *64-1550 Kamehameha Hwy (1 mile north of Wahiawa) Tel. 621-8408*
Daily 9am–5.30pm
Skip the gift shop (which is always clogged with slow-moving tourists clutching jumbo-sized drinks) and head instead to the pineapple fields, which bristle with thousands of spiny, stubby pineapple bushes. It's probably most interesting for pineapple fiends, but looking across the fields reminds the visitor of this imported fruit's economic and sociological importance in Hawaii.

Waimea Valley Audubon Center (**D** C2)
→ *59-864 Kamehameha Hwy Tel. 638 9199*
Center and Nature store open daily 9am–5pm
It boasts one restored *heiau* (the Hale O Lono, or House of Lono) and the ruins of several others, but the center's real draw is its hundreds of acres of strolling paths, hiking trails, world-class botanical gardens and, above all, Waimea Falls, a breathtaking 60-foot waterfall that pours into a cool natural pool.

Waimea Bay (**D** C2)
One of Hawaii's best and most popular swimming beaches, and one of the most famous surfing places ever as it holds the world record for the highest wave ever ridden, Waimea Bay boasts fine white sand and water as clear and blue and calm as a swimming pool in summer; in winter it has gigantic rollers.

Shark's Cove (**D** C2)
Hanauma Bay may be the best-known snorkeling spot, but real sealife enthusiasts flock to Shark's Cove, a rocky, initially inhospitable natural bay that's home to hundreds of candy-colored tropical fish, as well as sea cucumbers, corals, anemones, crabs and, best of all, graceful, gen sea turtles, whom you c swim alongside in the cool, clear waters.

Sunset Beach (**D** C1)
A gorgeous and picturesque stretch of beach, Sunset is a beach for the experienced swimmer and surfer only the tide is very strong, a even strong swimmers fi its pull difficult to fight. S what this beach lacks in aquatic accessibility is more than made up for i sheer theatricality, and there are few sights mor heart-stopping than watching the surfers tryi

DOLE
DOLE PLANTATION

WAIMEA FALLS

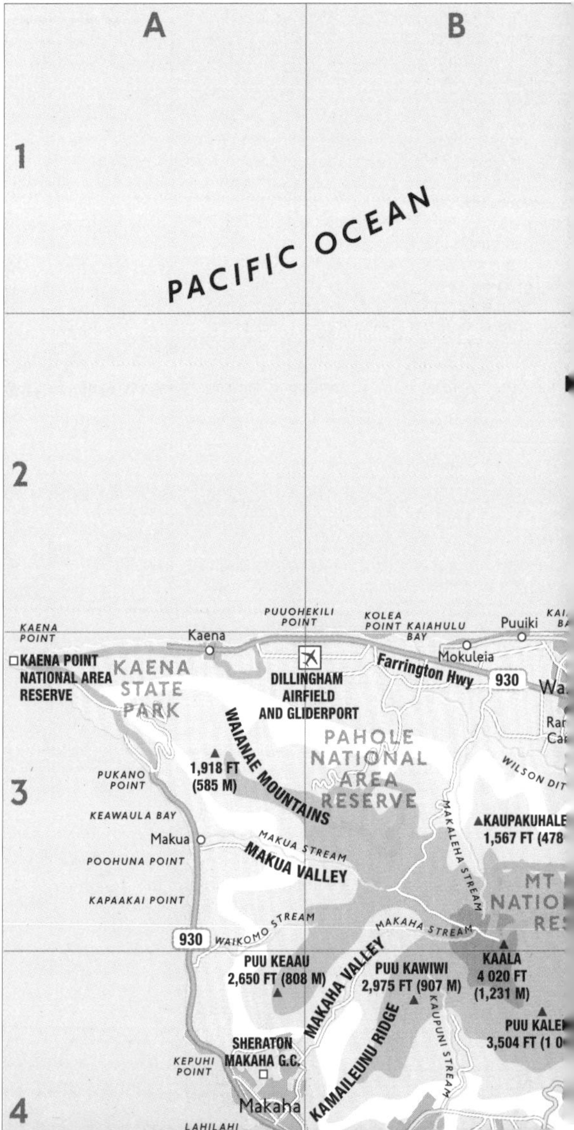
A
B
1
2
3
4
PACIFIC OCEAN
KAENA POINT
KAENA POINT NATIONAL AREA RESERVE
KAENA STATE PARK
Kaena
PUUOHEKILI POINT
KOLEA POINT
KAIAHULU BAY
Puuiki
Mokuleia
Farrington Hwy
930
DILLINGHAM AIRFIELD AND GLIDERPORT
PAHOLE NATIONAL AREA RESERVE
WAIANAE MOUNTAINS
1,918 FT (585 M)
PUKANO POINT
KEAWAULA BAY
Makua
POOHUNA POINT
MAKUA STREAM
MAKUA VALLEY
KAPAAKAI POINT
WAIKOMO STREAM
MAKALEHA STREAM
WILSON
KAUPAKUHALE
MAKAHA STREAM
KAALA 4 020 FT (1,231 M)
PUU KEAAU 2,650 FT (808 M)
MAKAHA VALLEY
PUU KAWIWI 2,975 FT (907 M)
KAUPUNI STREAM
KAMAILEUNU RIDGE
SHERATON MAKAHA G.C.
KEPUHI POINT
Makaha
LAHILAHI

For surfers – or mere surfing enthusiasts – Oahu's beautiful North Shore is the place to go. Oahuans consider this area 'the country' or 'the real Hawaii', and it's easy to see why. Although it's only a 45-minute-or-so drive from Honolulu, areas of it can feel like a step back in time, from the unsullied, sparkling beaches to the exuberant tangles of night-blooming cereus and the gnarled, windblown trees that jut from the cliffsides. Haleiwa, the North Shore's main town, is unavoidably touristy, but in such a good-natured, laid-back way that it's easier to just give in and do a little shopping before heading off to the nearest beach.

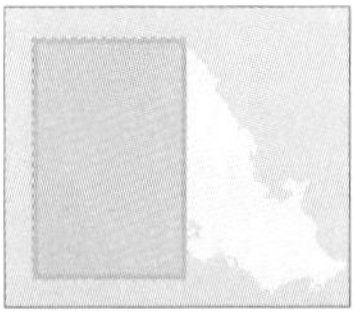

H.MIURA
H. MIURA SHAVE ICE

KUA AINA BURGERS

RESTAURANTS

Kua Aina Burgers (**D** C2)
→ 66-214 Kamehameha Hwy, Haleiwa Tel. 637-6067 Daily 11am–8pm
There's a Waikiki satellite (and a Tokyo one too!), but somehow Kua Aina's juicy, charred burgers taste best just before or after a long swim in Waimea Bay. The place is always packed, but the line moves fast. $5.

Waialua Bakery (**D** C2)
→ 66-200 Kamehameha Hwy, Haleiwa Tel. 637-9079 Mon-Sat 9am–4pm
Fresh breads, sandwiches, fruits, smoothies (and fresh-baked cookies, muffins and pound cake) abound at this breezy, casual bakery-cum-café, a favorite of locals and tourists alike. About $7 for a sandwich, cookie and drink.

Café Haleiwa (**D** C2)
→ 66-460 Kamehameha Hwy, Haleiwa Tel. 637-5516 Daily 7am–2pm
Unlike many of Haleiwa's famous haunts, this is a favorite of locals and tourists alike, who flock to this woodframe eatery for its generous, fresh breakfasts and lunches, as well as strong cups of Kona coffee. In the late morning, you can eavesdrop on surfers earnestly discussing the day's waves. $5–$10.

Haleiwa Joe's (**D** C2)
→ 66-011 Kamehameha Hwy, Haleiwa Tel. 637-8005 Sun-Thu 11.30am–9.30pm (10.30pm Fri-Sat)
Next to Anahulu Stream Bridge, overlooking the marina (and some spectacular late-afternoon sunsets) is the area's de facto fine-dining establishment. The food (*ono*, *opakapaka*, crabmeat spring rolls; *ahi poke* – cubes of fish marinated in a powerful soy sauce; steaks, coconut-battered fried shrimp) is fresh, flavorful and thoughtful without veering into pretension, and Joe's itself, with its deep wood deck and friendly service, is the perfect place to enjoy it. $13–$39.

Jameson's by the Sea (**D** C2)
→ 62-540 Kamehameha Hwy, Haleiwa Tel. 637-4336 Mon-Tue 5–9pm; Sat-Sun 11am–9pm; Upstairs: Wed-Sun 5–9pm
Another seaside mainstay, the romantic, cozy Jameson's has become something of a North Shore destination, both for its ambience and its

Cafe
HALEIWA
AIR-CONDITIONED
ALEIWA

WAIALUA
BAKERY
Juice bar
WAIALUA BAKERY

SURF N SEA

flavorful cuisine. And while Jameson's steak is reliably delicious, the fish (especially *opakapaka* served with scallions and crabmeat, or the salmon spread) is what you should go for. $17–$22.

ICE CREAM

Matsumoto Shave Ice (**D** C2)
→ *66-087 Kamehameha Hwy, Haleiwa Tel. 637-4827*
H. Miura Shave Ice (**D** C2)
→ *66-057 Kamehameha Hwy, Haleiwa Tel. 637-4845*
Both: daily 9am–6pm
People in Hawaii are serious about their shave ice, and although only a few yards separate Miura's and Matsumoto's, each has their loyalists eager to extol the virtues of their favorite North Shore shave ice stand. Matsumoto's, the more famous of the two, is known for their super-fine, almost slushy, shave and generous drenchings of syrup, as well as their witty and inventive merchandise. Miura's, which attracts more locals than tourists, has a slightly grainier shave. Try a cone at each ($2.50 for a cone).

SHOPPING

Global Creations (**D** C2)
→ *66-079 Kamehameha Hwy, Haleiwa Tel. 637-1505*
Daily 10am–6pm
Decorated – like many of Haleiwa's stores – in a spirited tropical-meets-Southeast Asian motif, this welcoming store sells home decorations, whimsical knickknacks, throw pillows and soaps and perfumes.

Bali Moon (**D** C2)
→ *66-200 Kamehameha Hwy, Haleiwa Tel. 637-0012*
Daily 10.15am–6.15pm
This cozy quasi-Balinese shop has dark wood floors, a cheerful staff and racks of lightweight, bright-colored cotton sarongs and wraps, and stacks of woven cotton rugs and slip dresses.

Strong Current (**D** C2)
→ *66-208 Kamehameha Hwy, Haleiwa Tel. 637-3410*
Daily 10.20am–6.45pm
A cheerful, tourist-friendly store packed with everything the budding surfer manqué might need, including T-shirts, flip-flops, swimsuits, sarongs and of course kitschy postcards and hula dolls.

Tropical Rush (**D** C2)
→ *62-620A Kamehameha Hwy, Haleiwa*
Tel. 637-8886
Daily 9am–7pm
Surf N Sea (**D** C2)
→ *62-595 Kamehameha Hwy, Haleiwa Tel. 637-9887*
Daily 9am–7pm
You'll find plenty of Honolulu tourists exclaiming over the accessories and surfing gear at these two cheek-by-jowl stores. Tropical Rush, the smaller of the two, sells its own line of sharp and witty T-shirts, as well as one-of-a-kind bikinis, board shorts, a limited selection of longboards, and shorts and sarongs (the store has frequent sales of the latter). Across the street, the much more extensive Surf N Sea sells beach fashion, swimsuits, jewelry, stickers and flip-flops (mostly for the young and hip). Also a wide selection of body boards, longboards and scuba and snorkeling equipment.

Patagonia (**D** C2)
→ *66-250 Kamehameha Hwy, Haleiwa Tel. 637-1245*
Daily 10am–6pm
The Hawaii outpost of this California-based chain sells all its signature goods – capilene underwear, microfiber tights and fleece jackets – as well as an extended swimwear collection, and logo T-shirts made especially for the store.

North Shore Marketplace (**D** C2)
→ *66-250 Kamehameha Hwy, Haleiwa*

Polynesian Treasures
→ *Tel. 637-1288 Mon-Sat 10am–6pm (5pm Sun)*
Kitsch abounds in this jam-packed jumble of a store, but it's pretty much irresistible. A good place to load up on all the touristy souvenirs – koa jewelry, bright Hawaiian fabrics, papery hula skirts, cheap, plinky ukuleles – your friends back home won't want to admit they're expecting. There are also some unexpected treasures, including woven *lauhala* bags, bone fishhook jewelry, and homemade weapons from across Polynesia.

Oceans in Glass Gallery
→ *Tel. 637-3366*
Daily 10am–6pm
This cheerful, knockabout wood and glass studio-cum-store looks straight out of southern California, but the glass sculptures (many with a sealife motif) are pure Hawaii. There's a good deal of corny stuff here but some nice simple pieces as well.

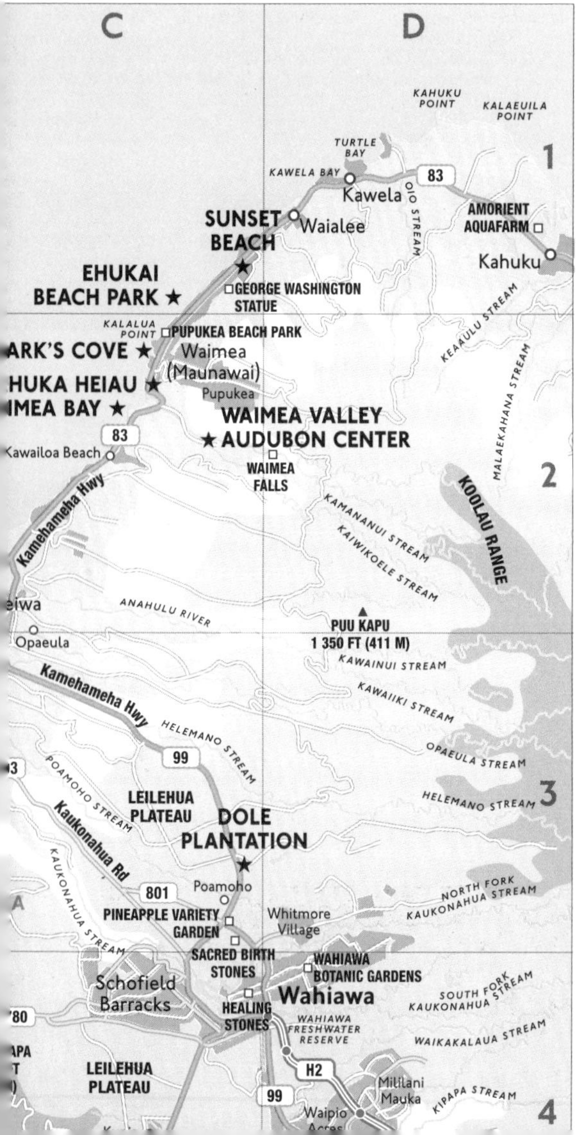
C
D
KAHUKU POINT
KALAEUILA POINT
TURTLE BAY
KAWELA BAY
Kawela
83
OIO STREAM
AMORIENT AQUAFARM
Kahuku
SUNSET BEACH
Waialee
EHUKAI BEACH PARK
GEORGE WASHINGTON STATUE
KALALUA POINT
PUPUKEA BEACH PARK
KEAAULU STREAM
MALAEKAHANA STREAM
ARK'S COVE
Waimea (Maunawai)
HUKA HEIAU
Pupukea
IMEA BAY
WAIMEA VALLEY AUDUBON CENTER
Kawailoa Beach
WAIMEA FALLS
KOOLAU RANGE
Kamehameha Hwy
KAMANANUI STREAM
KAIWIKOELE STREAM
ANAHULU RIVER
PUU KAPU
1 350 FT (411 M)
Opaeula
KAWAINUI STREAM
KAWAIIKI STREAM
HELEMANO STREAM
OPAEULA STREAM
99
POAMOHO STREAM
LEILEHUA PLATEAU
DOLE PLANTATION
Kaukonahua Rd
801
Poamoho
NORTH FORK KAUKONAHUA STREAM
PINEAPPLE VARIETY GARDEN
Whitmore Village
KAUKONAHUA STREAM
SACRED BIRTH STONES
WAHIAWA BOTANIC GARDENS
Schofield Barracks
Wahiawa
HEALING STONES
SOUTH FORK KAUKONAHUA STREAM
WAHIAWA FRESHWATER RESERVE
WAIKAKALAUA STREAM
H2
Mililani Mauka
KIPAPA STREAM
Waipio Acres
1
2
3
4

SUNSET BEACH

PUUOMAHUKA HEIAU

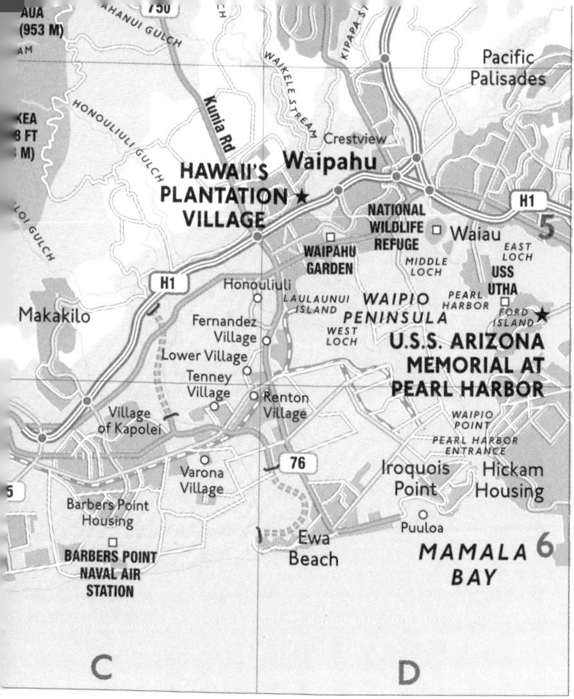
(953 M)
HONOULIULI GULCH
WAIKELE STREAM
KIPAPA ST
Kunia Rd
Pacific
Palisades
Crestview
Waipahu
HAWAII'S
PLANTATION
VILLAGE
H1
NATIONAL
WILDLIFE
REFUGE
Waiau
EAST
LOCH
WAIPAHU
GARDEN
MIDDLE
LOCH
USS
UTHA
H1
Honouliuli
LAULAUNUI
ISLAND
WAIPIO
PENINSULA
PEARL
HARBOR
FORD
ISLAND
Makakilo
Fernandez
Village
WEST
LOCH
U.S.S. ARIZONA
MEMORIAL AT
PEARL HARBOR
Lower Village
Tenney
Village
Renton
Village
Village
of Kapolei
WAIPIO
POINT
PEARL HARBOR
ENTRANCE
76
Varona
Village
Iroquois
Point
Hickam
Housing
Barbers Point
Housing
Puuloa
Ewa
Beach
BARBERS POINT
NAVAL AIR
STATION
MAMALA
BAY
5
6
C
D

U.S.S. *ARIZONA* PEARL HARBOR

THE NORTH SHORE LANDSCAPE

…e Sunset's towering …s.

…kai Beach Park (**D** C1)
…you've had your fill …citement from Sunset, …ways nice to retreat …the beach to Ehukai, …e you can spread out …e beach before …shing about in the …paratively placid waters.

…omahuka Heiau (**D** C2)
…amehameha Hwy past …nea Beach Park, toward …kea
…well-preserved, long …low-walled *heiau* …ple), probably dating …to the early 17th …ury, is a national …rical site. Hawaiians still bring offerings of fruit to the small altar. It's worth driving up here for the superb views the *heiau* affords of Waimea Valley and the bay.

Hawaii's Plantation Village (**D** D5)
→ *94-695 Waipahu St, in Waipahu Tel. 677-0110 Mon-Fri 9am–3pm; Sat 10am–3pm. Tours every hour on the hour*
From the mid-1840s through the mid-1940s, Hawaii was essentially a series of large plantations, a backwater agricultural territory. But although the pineapple and sugar industries abruptly lost much of their influence and power in Hawaii's rapid modernization, their contributions to the state's social development are unignorable. The companies' labor pools alone – from Korea, China, Japan, the Philippines, Puerto Rico and Portugal – populated Hawaii, and many contemporary residents are descendants of those first waves of laborers. This fascinating living museum re-creates a sugar plantation's living quarters, and offers provocative clues about the development of Hawaii's unique hodgepodge culture.

U.S.S. *Arizona* Memorial at Pearl Harbor (**D** D5)
→ *1 Arizona Memorial Drive, Tel. 422-0561*
Daily 7.30am–5pm
One of Hawaii's most popular tourist destinations is the U.S.S. *Arizona* Memorial, which floats above the ship whose obliteration in December 1941 spurned America to enter the fray of World War II. Also in the harbor is the U.S.S. *Missouri* (or 'Mighty Mo'), a battleship that saw action in the battles of Iwo Jima and Okinawa, as well as the Korean and 1991 Gulf wars. It is now a museum ship.

HAWAII VISITORS BUREAU MARKER
PACIFIC TSUNAMI MUSEUM
PACIFIC TSUNAMI MUSEUM

RAINBOW FALLS

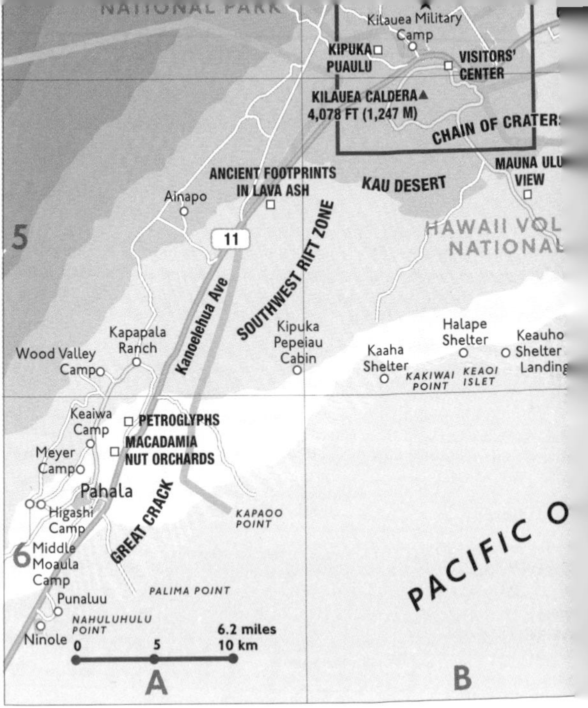
Kilauea Military Camp
KIPUKA PUAULU
VISITORS' CENTER
KILAUEA CALDERA
4,078 FT (1,247 M)
CHAIN OF CRATERS
ANCIENT FOOTPRINTS IN LAVA ASH
KAU DESERT
MAUNA ULU VIEW
Ainapo
5
11
SOUTHWEST RIFT ZONE
HAWAII VOL
NATIONAL
Kanoelehua Ave
Kapapala Ranch
Wood Valley Camp
Kipuka Pepeiau Cabin
Kaaha Shelter
Halape Shelter
Keauhou Shelter Landing
KAKIWAI POINT
KEAOI ISLET
Keaiwa Camp
PETROGLYPHS
MACADAMIA NUT ORCHARDS
Meyer Camp
Pahala
Higashi Camp
GREAT CRACK
KAPAOO POINT
6
Middle Moaula Camp
PALIMA POINT
PACIFIC O
Punaluu
NAHULUHULU POINT
Ninole
0
5
6.2 miles
10 km
A
B

Lyman Museum (**E** D1)
→ *276 Haili St*
Tel. 935-5021
Mon-Sat 9.30am–4.30pm
Built in 1839 by the Lymans, an early missionary couple, this wood-frame, low-ceilinged house was restored in the 1930s and later declared a historic landmark. The adjoining Lyman Museum building displays some of the Lymans' treasures and collectibles, as well as rotating exhibits about Hawaii flora and fauna.

Hilo Bay / Coconut Island / Liliuokalani Gardens (**E** C3)
If Hilo has a shortcoming, it is its lack of appealing beaches. Still, it's worth visiting Hilo Bay, a long stretch of grayish water that runs the length of downtown. Have a picnic near Liliuokalani Gardens, a sweet – if somewhat twee – Japanese garden, and then stroll over the narrow arched bridge to Coconut Island, a small patch of land that seems to float near the bay's edge.

Pacific Tsunami Museum (**E** D1)
→ *130 Kamehameha Ave*
Tel. 935-0926
Mon-Sat 9am–4pm
The museum is dedicated to the 1946 and 1960 tsunamis that devastated Hilo, and which were huge setbacks to the city and its inhabitants, causing vast economic and social restructuring. There are oral histories from the survivors, who offer excellent insights into the town's character and sociology.

Boiling Pots / Rainbow Falls (**E** C3)
→ *Head toward the mountains on Waianuenue Ave, take the right fork after the 1-mile marker and follow the signs to Rainbow Falls. The Boiling Pots are a mile farther uphill.*
These are two of Hilo's most impressive natural wonders. Rainbow Falls is a bright, wide splash waterfall, flanked by sh of ferns and magnificer greenery, and Boiling P a little farther uphill, is series of smaller waterf and natural pools of bubbling, swirling freshwater.

Mauna Loa Macadam Nut Farm (**E** C3)
→ *Drive south on Hwy 11 about 10 minutes and lo for signs; the plantation on the left Tel. 982-656*
Daily 8.30am–5.30pm
Macadamia nuts aren't native to Hawaii, but they've become one of enduring symbols of th

LYMAN MUSEUM

HILO BAY FROM COCONUT ISLAND

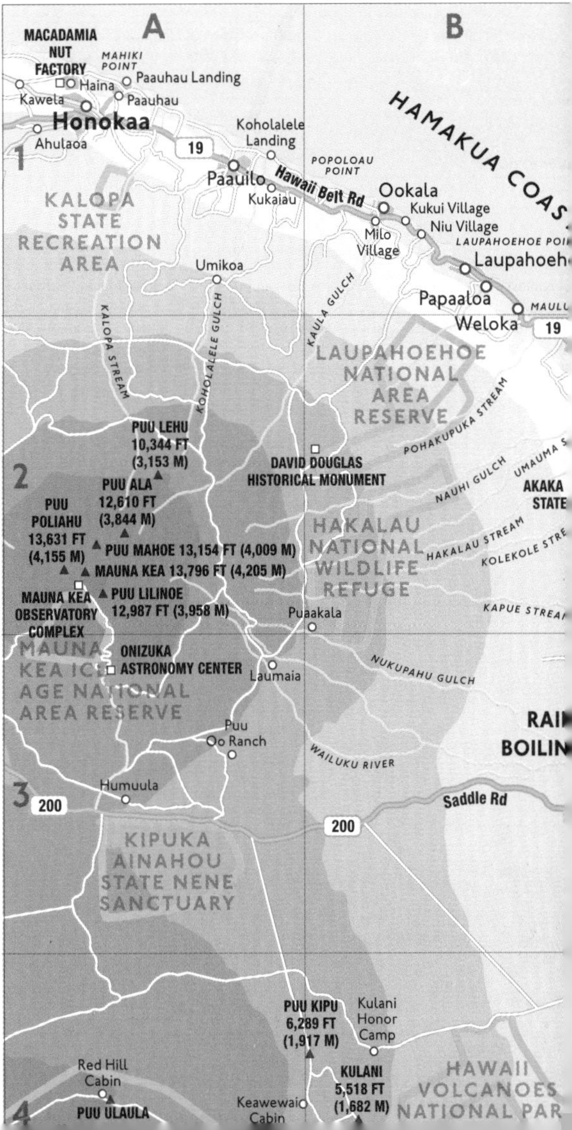
A
B
1
2
3
4
MACADAMIA NUT FACTORY
MAHIKI POINT
Haina
Paauhau Landing
Kawela
Paauhau
Honokaa
Ahulaoa
19
Koholalele Landing
POPOLOAU POINT
Paauilo
Kukaiau
Hawaii Belt Rd
HAMAKUA COAS
Ookala
Kukui Village
Niu Village
Milo Village
LAUPAHOEHOE POI
Laupahoeh
Papaaloa
Weloka
MAULU
KALOPA STATE RECREATION AREA
Umikoa
KALOPA STREAM
KOHOLALELE GULCH
KAULA GULCH
LAUPAHOEHOE NATIONAL AREA RESERVE
POHAKUPUKA STREAM
PUU LEHU 10,344 FT (3,153 M)
DAVID DOUGLAS HISTORICAL MONUMENT
NAUHI GULCH
UMAUMA S
AKAKA STATE
PUU ALA 12,610 FT (3,844 M)
PUU POLIAHU 13,631 FT (4,155 M)
PUU MAHOE 13,154 FT (4,009 M)
MAUNA KEA 13,796 FT (4,205 M)
HAKALAU NATIONAL WILDLIFE REFUGE
HAKALAU STREAM
KOLEKOLE STRE
MAUNA KEA OBSERVATORY COMPLEX
PUU LILINOE 12,987 FT (3,958 M)
Puaakala
KAPUE STREA
MAUNA KEA ICE AGE NATIONAL AREA RESERVE
ONIZUKA ASTRONOMY CENTER
Laumaia
NUKUPAHU GULCH
RAI
BOILIN
Puu Oo Ranch
WAILUKU RIVER
Humuula
200
Saddle Rd
KIPUKA AINAHOU STATE NENE SANCTUARY
PUU KIPU 6,289 FT (1,917 M)
Kulani Honor Camp
Red Hill Cabin
KULANI 5,518 FT (1,682 M)
HAWAII VOLCANOES NATIONAL PAR
PUU ULAULA
Keawewai Cabin

Big Island tourists may flock to Kailua-Kona's plush resorts and glittering beaches, but for a taste of real Hawaii, there's no better place to visit than sleepy, easygoing Hilo. The wettest city in America, Hilo (which receives around 130 inches of rain annually) is known and loved throughout the state for its lush foliage, old-fashioned charm, small-town eclecticism, and spectacular farmers' market, where you can buy just-picked mangoes by the bagful and bunches of orchids for a dollar.

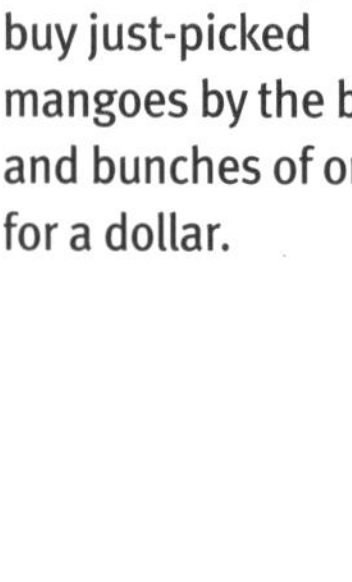

RESTAURANT KAIKODO

sig zane desig

SIG ZANE DESIGNS

RESTAURANTS

Nori's (**E** D1)
→ *688 Kinoole St, Suite 124*
Tel. 935-9133
Sun-Mon 10.30am–9.30pm; Tue-Sat 10.30am–3pm, 4pm–midnight (1am Fri-Sat)
This is a cheerful, scabby one-room mom-and-pop restaurant with friendly service and fantastic local food, including terrific saimin (topped with wonton, *char siu*, extra fishcake or *shiso* flavoring), mahimahi sandwiches and an old island favorite: loco moco (a beef – or *ahi* – patty over rice with a sunny-side-up egg and lots of gravy). À la carte $8.

Ocean Sushi Deli (**E** D1)
→ *239 Keawe St*
Tel. 961-6625 Mon-Sat 10–2pm, 4.30–9pm
The lumps of sometimes crudely shaped sushi at this linoleum-floored deli may not look like the elegant constructions you're used to, but they'll probably taste a whole lot better. Ocean Sushi's fish is so fresh it melts in your mouth. À la carte $15.

Seaside Restaurant (**E** C3)
→ *1790 Kalanianaole Ave*
Tel. 935-8825
Tue-Thu, Sun 5–8.30pm (9pm Fri-Sat)
Hilo's favorite restaurant is located in a shack surrounded by freshwater fish ponds. The mullet from these ponds is the Seaside's signature dish: two fish are flash-sautéed, Chinese-style, with garlic and cilantro. Excellent as well are the mahimahi, ahi and black cod. And save room for the bread pudding, which comes studded with chunks of soft purple taro root and sticky with cream. Reserve ahead. À la carte $19.

Restaurant Kaikodo (**E** D1)
→ *62 Keawe St*
Tel. 961-2558 Daily 11am–2.30pm, 5–9.30pm
Hilo's only high-end restaurant, a high-ceilinged former bank, can hold its own against any big-city eatery. It serves memorable farmers'-market-fresh cuisine (a peppers-and-mushroom appetizer is followed by *opakapaka* in a vegetable pistou). The owners, Asian antiquities dealers, have decorated the space with beautiful scrolls, screens and heaps of orchids. There are plans to convert the second floor into a

ON MAMA

HANA HOU

HILO FARMERS' MARKET

gallery. Reserve ahead. À la carte $23.

ICE CREAM, CANDIES

Hilo Homemade Ice Cream (**E** C3)
→ *1651 Ainaola Drive*
Tel. 959-5959
Mon-Sat 10.30am–5pm
The sweet treats from this privately owned ice cream factory are the perfect antidote to a humid day. Particularly delicious are such flavors as macadamia nut, poha berry, and Kona coffee. The green tea is also exceptionally flavorful.

Big Island Candies (**E** C3)
→ *585 Hinano St*
Tel. 935-8890
Daily 8.30am–5pm
Spacious factory-cum-shop, where you can watch workers hand-dip shortbread into vats of chocolate. You can buy boxes of chocolate-covered shortbread cookies, and, for the more adventurous, chocolate-dipped squid legs and soy sauce peanuts; the store will ship anywhere.

Two Ladies' Kitchen (**E** D1)
→ *274 Kilauea Ave*
Tel. 961-4766
Wed-Sat 11am–6pm
Two Ladies' has the reputation of making the best *mochi* in the islands; they certainly make the prettiest. Buy boxes of pastel-colored rounds of rice cake dough dusted with snowy rice flour and filled with traditional (red bean) or more experimental pastes. Count on placing your order a day in advance, and make sure to enjoy these sweets fresh.

SHOPPING

Dragon Mama (**E** C3)
→ *266 Kamehameha Ave*
Tel. 934-9081 Mon-Fri 9am–5pm (4pm Sat)
You can spend hours in this fabric store with its eclectic and beautiful selection of Japanese kimonos and textiles, from bolts of indigo-dyed waxed cotton to yards of colorful, finely woven wools. The store is best known for their futons, which are made with buckwheat filling and sewn by hand.

Oshima's Antiques (**E** D1)
→ *202 Kamehameha Ave*
Tel. 969-1554
Mon-Sat 10am–5pm
More of a junk shop, but a colorful and eclectic one, with some real treasures – both kitsch and genuine – including affordable, persimmon-orange lacquerware, old carved wooden bowls, textiles, ivory jewelry and a cheerful set of Pyrex nesting bowls decorated with orange and pink spangles.

Sig Zane Designs (**E** C3)
→ *29 Shipman St*
Tel. 935-9980
Mon-Fri 9am–6pm
Colorful cotton dresses, bags, slippers and aloha shirts in Zane's bold signature prints, many of which are wildly inventive and original graphic riffs on traditional Hawaiian prints and designs.

Hana Hou (**E** D1)
→ *164 Kamehameha Ave*
Tel. 935-4555
Mon-Fri 9am–5.30pm; Sat 9.30am–4.30pm
This welcoming, narrow wedge of a store – owned by Sig Zane's sister – captures Hilo's warmth and artistic style. Besides the collection of women's shirts, dresses, and cheongsams in retro-printed silks, there's also a wide selection of tchotchkes, bamboo and silver jewelry and local company Island Botanicals' sumptuous, tropical-scented lotions, balms and soaps.

Basically Books (**E** D1)
→ *160 Kamehameha Ave*
Tel. 961-0144
Mon-Sat 9am–5pm; Sun 10am–3pm
Along with a wide selection of Hawaiiana books (including novels, histories and flora and fauna guidebooks), stuffed animals and notecards, this bookstore specializes in maps, particularly those of the Hawaiian islands.

Hilo Farmers' Market (**E** D1)
→ *Corner of Kamehameha and Mamo Sts*
Tel. 933-1000
Wed and Sat, year-round, 'from dawn till it's gone'
One of the most colorful farmers' markets anywhere, and one of the most diverse. One side is dedicated to farmers selling all produce – dried *ahi*, proteas, heliconias, lychee, mangoes, avocados – and the other to local crafts people. Much on offer is scandalously cheap – you can buy a small sackful of papayas and an armful of orchids for five dollars.

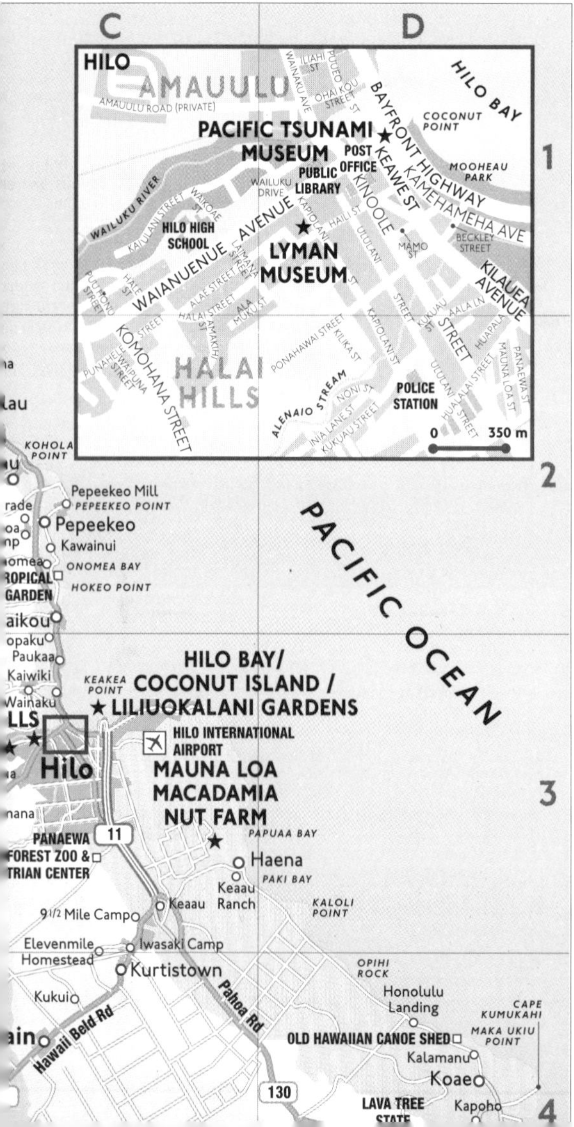
C
D
1
2
3
4
HILO
AMAUULU
AMAUULU ROAD (PRIVATE)
PACIFIC TSUNAMI MUSEUM
POST OFFICE
PUBLIC LIBRARY
HILO BAY
COCONUT POINT
MOOHEAU PARK
BAYFRONT HIGHWAY
KAMEHAMEHA AVE
KEAWE ST
KINOOLE
WAILUKU RIVER
WAILUKU DRIVE
HILO HIGH SCHOOL
WAIANUENUE AVENUE
LYMAN MUSEUM
KAPIOLANI
HAILI ST
ULULANI
MAMO ST
BECKLEY STREET
KILAUEA AVENUE
KOMOHANA STREET
HALAI HILLS
PONAHAWAI STREET
KILIKA ST
ALENAIO STREAM
NONI ST
INIA LANE ST
KUKUAU STREET
POLICE STATION
HUALALAI STREET
MAUNA LOA ST
PANAEWA ST
0 350 m
KOHOLA POINT
Pepeekeo Mill
PEPEEKEO POINT
Pepeekeo
Kawainui
ONOMEA BAY
HOKEO POINT
PACIFIC OCEAN
HILO BAY/ COCONUT ISLAND / LILIUOKALANI GARDENS
KEAKEA POINT
Kaiwiki
Wainaku
HILO INTERNATIONAL AIRPORT
Hilo
MAUNA LOA MACADAMIA NUT FARM
PAPUAA BAY
11
Haena
Keaau Ranch
PAKI BAY
Keaau
KALOLI POINT
9 1/2 Mile Camp
Elevenmile Homestead
Iwasaki Camp
Kurtistown
Pahoa Rd
OPIHI ROCK
Honolulu Landing
CAPE KUMUKAHI
Kukui
Hawaii Beld Rd
OLD HAWAIIAN CANOE SHED
MAKA UKIU POINT
Kalamanu
Koae
130
LAVA TREE STATE
Kapoho

MAUNA LOA MACADAMIA NUT FARM

MACADAMIA NUTS

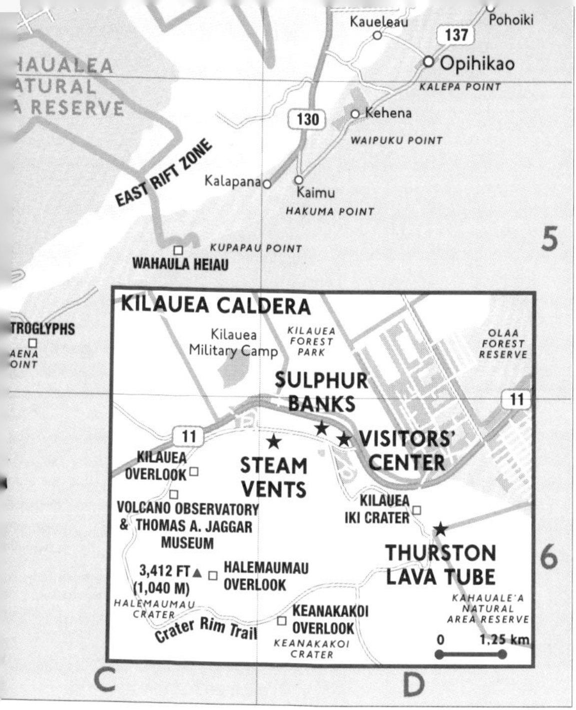
Kaueleau
Pohoiki
137
Opihikao
KALEPA POINT
AUALEA
ATURAL
A RESERVE
130
Kehena
WAIPUKU POINT
EAST RIFT ZONE
Kalapana
Kaimu
HAKUMA POINT
5
KUPAPAU POINT
WAHAULA HEIAU
KILAUEA CALDERA
TROGLYPHS
AENA
OINT
Kilauea
Military Camp
KILAUEA
FOREST
PARK
OLAA
FOREST
RESERVE
SULPHUR
BANKS
11
11
VISITORS'
CENTER
KILAUEA
OVERLOOK
STEAM
VENTS
VOLCANO OBSERVATORY
& THOMAS A. JAGGAR
MUSEUM
KILAUEA
IKI CRATER
THURSTON
LAVA TUBE
6
3,412 FT
(1,040 M)
HALEMAUMAU
OVERLOOK
HALEMAUMAU
CRATER
KAHAUALE'A
NATURAL
AREA RESERVE
Crater Rim Trail
KEANAKAKOI
OVERLOOK
KEANAKAKOI
CRATER
0
1,25 km
C
D

SULPHUR BANKS STEAM VENTS

THURSTON LAVA TUBE

ds. Mauna Loa's
ors' center, located on
ip of its lush, verdant
tation, is worth a visit
for its gorgeous nature
k as well as its factory
e, where visitors can
ge on rich, buttery
colate-smothered nuts.

waii Volcanoes
ional Park (**E** B4-5)
el. 985-6000
y 24 hrs, year-round
.nps.gov/havo/index.htm
fascinating 377-
are-mile park, which
udes the active volcano
uea, the massive, now
nct Mauna Loa, and
y natural and man-
de wonders, is a must-see. The park maintains a helpful website with information about the day's lava flow, safety precautions, history and camping regulations. You can also find information about the park's many hiking trails, including one through the Kilauea Caldera. Here are some destinations worth special consideration.

Visitors' Center (**E** D6)
→ *Tel. 967-7311*
Daily 7.45am–5pm
Thomas A. Jaggar Museum
Tel. 967-7643
Daily 8.30am–5pm
A good place to begin a volcano adventure, the Visitors' Center offers a brief film, a bookstore and a small museum. The daily schedule of ranger-led walks and talks is posted at 9am. Thomas Jaggar Museum, about 3 miles away, offers a breathtaking view of the caldera, as well as displays about Kilauea's natural wonders and its religious significance to the ancient Hawaiians, who considered the volcano a sacred place.

Sulphur Banks and Steam Vents (**E** D6)
One of the first sights you'll see off the well-trod Crater Rim Trail is the Sulphur Banks and Steam Vents, two of the park's many natural oddities, and certainly one of its more unique sensuous experiences. Trails of white steam wheeze out of the parched ground like ghosts, but while the pure steam smells as clean as it looks, the sulphur fumes smell like rotting eggs.

Thurston Lava Tube (**E** D6)
A damp and slightly eerie natural cave formed by lava. The Thurston Lava Tube, only part of which is open to the public, is heavily trafficked but worth a visit, if only for its unearthly quiet and cool.

HULIHEE PALACE

NAPOOPOO BEACH PARK

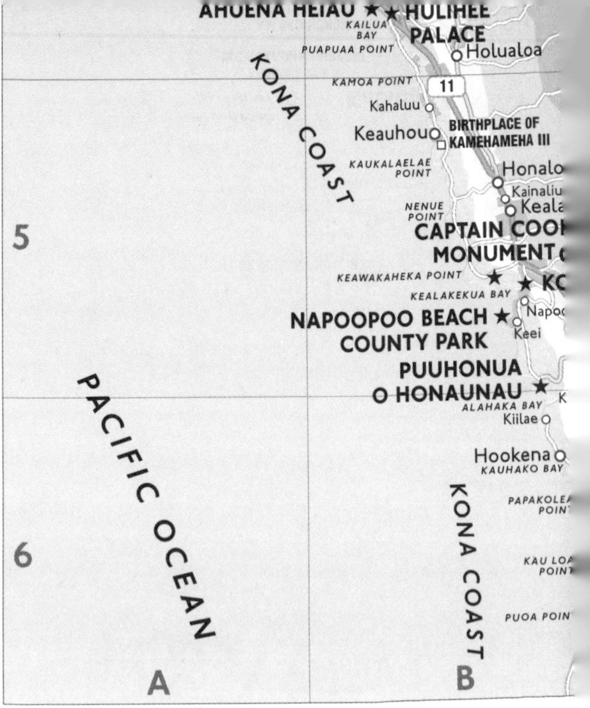
AHUENA HEIAU
HULIHEE PALACE
KAILUA BAY
PUAPUAA POINT
Holualoa
KONA COAST
KAMOA POINT
11
Kahaluu
Keauhou
BIRTHPLACE OF KAMEHAMEHA III
KAUKALAELAE POINT
NENUE POINT
CAPTAIN COOK MONUMENT
KEAWAKAHEKA POINT
KEALAKEKUA BAY
NAPOOPOO BEACH COUNTY PARK
Keei
PUUHONUA O HONAUNAU
ALAHAKA BAY
Kiilae
Hookena
KAUHAKO BAY
PACIFIC OCEAN
KONA COAST
5
6
A
B

Parker Ranch Visitor Center and Museum (**F** A1)
→ *Parker Ranch Center, Kamuela Tel. 885-7655 Mon-Sat 9am–5pm; Museum closes at 4pm; Wagon tours Tue-Sat 10am–2pm*
This ranch owns about 10 percent of the Big Island's land and is one of the largest ranches in the United States. After a visit to the gift store (see previous page), stop by the Visitor Center, where you can wander through the adjacent museum and watch a short, fascinating film about Hawaii's long ranching traditions. Established in 1847, it still employs 15 full-time *paniolos* (Hawaiian for cowboys). Finally, take the covered-wagon tour through part of the ranch's holdings.

Kamuela Museum (**F** C2)
→ *Junction of Hwy 19 and Hwy 250, Kamuela Tel. 885-4724 Daily 8am– 5pm*
Less a traditional museum than a bizarre and delightful cabinet-of-wonders, this tiny mom-and-pop venture displays all manner of ancient Hawaiian weaponry, crafts and instruments alongside 'antiquities' of dubious provenance and intrinsic worth. It's all fun, though, and curated with verve and idiosyncrasy.

Puako Petroglyph Park (**F** B2-3)
Between the Orchid at Mauna Lani and the Holoholo Kai Beach Park parking lot
Petroglyph fields dot large sections of the Kailua-Kona coast, but Puako is one of the most famous. Carved onto the smooth sides of lava stone are symbols for men, children, dogs and women as well as abstract and inscrutable markings.

Hulihee Palace (**F** B4)
→ *75-5718 Alii Drive, Kailua-Kona Tel. 329-1877 Mon-Fri 9am–4pm (10am Sat-Sun)*
This lava-wood-and-co structure, built in 1838 Governor John Adams Kuakini, played host to Hawaiian dignitaries a royalty on their trips to Kailua-Kona. There are some priceless artifact display here, including feather cape, as well as some breathtaking furniture made from gleaming native hardw

Ahuena Heiau (**F** B4)
→ *At Kailua Bay*
Another *heiau*, this one dedicated to the Hawai god Lono. Like many *heiaus* across the islan this one has been recon structed by archeologis

PARKER RANCH

KAMUELA MUSEUM

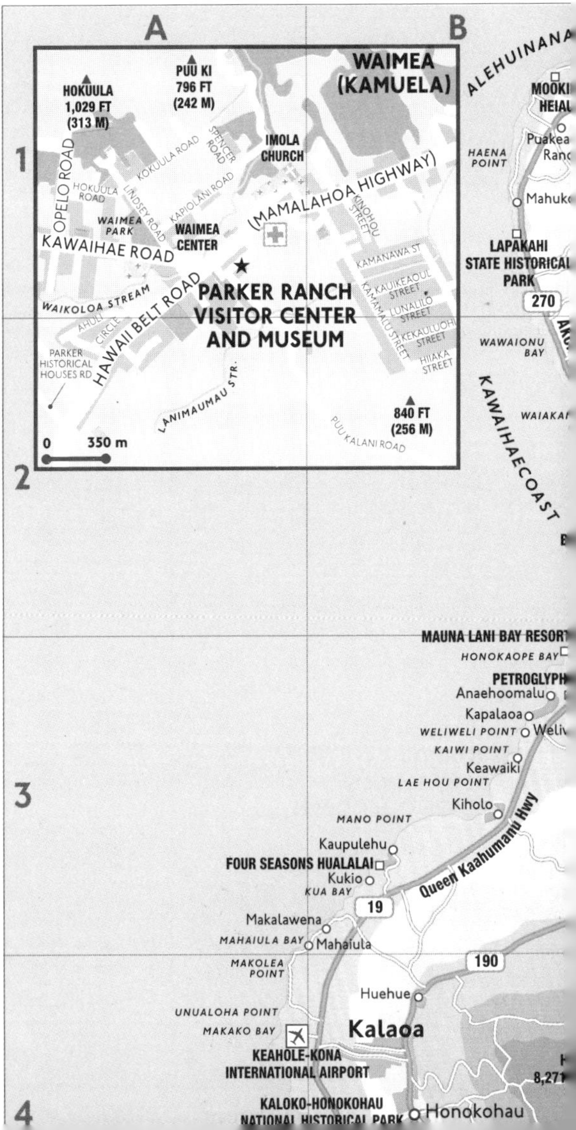
A
B
1
2
3
4
WAIMEA (KAMUELA)
HOKUULA 1,029 FT (313 M)
PUU KI 796 FT (242 M)
IMOLA CHURCH
OPELO ROAD
KOKUULA ROAD
SPENCER ROAD
HOKUULA ROAD
LINDSEY ROAD
KAPIOLANI ROAD
(MAMALAHOA HIGHWAY)
KINOHOU STREET
WAIMEA PARK
WAIMEA CENTER
KAWAIHAE ROAD
KAMANAWA ST
KAUIKEAOUL STREET
LUNALILO STREET
KAMAMALU STREET
KEKAULUOHI STREET
HIIAKA STREET
WAIKOLOA STREAM
AHULI CIRCLE
HAWAII BELT ROAD
PARKER RANCH VISITOR CENTER AND MUSEUM
PARKER HISTORICAL HOUSES RD
LANIMAUMAU STR.
840 FT (256 M)
PUU KALANI ROAD
0
350 m
ALEHUINANA
HAENA POINT
Puakea
Mahuk
LAPAKAHI STATE HISTORICAL PARK
270
WAWAIONU BAY
KAWAIHAE COAST
MAUNA LANI BAY RESORT
HONOKAOPE BAY
PETROGLYPH
Anaehoomalu
Kapalaoa
WELIWELI POINT
KAIWI POINT
Keawaiki
LAE HOU POINT
Kiholo
MANO POINT
Kaupulehu
FOUR SEASONS HUALALAI
Kukio
KUA BAY
Queen Kaahumanu Hwy
19
Makalawena
MAHAIULA BAY
Mahaiula
MAKOLEA POINT
190
Huehue
UNUALOHA POINT
MAKAKO BAY
Kalaoa
KEAHOLE-KONA INTERNATIONAL AIRPORT
KALOKO-HONOKOHAU NATIONAL HISTORICAL PARK
Honokohau

Big Island – Kamuela and Kailua-Kona

The Big Island's beautiful Kailua-Kona coast is best known for its long stretches of glittering beaches and luxury hotels, but the area is also home to a number of historical and sacred sites, including the haunting City of Refuge. Inland and to the north lies cool, breezy Kamuela (also known as Waimea). There are dozens of small cattle and pig ranchers here, but the area is dominated by the sprawling Parker Ranch, whose cows graze in the shadow of the mist-shrouded Kohala Mountains.

MERRIMAN'S

DANIEL THIEBAU

RESTAURANTS

Tako Taco (**F** A1)
→ *65-1271 Kawaihae Rd, Kamuela Tel. 887-1717 Daily 11am–8pm*
As the name implies (*tako* means octopus in Japanese), this tiny place gives tacos an original, Asian-inspired riff, substituting remarkably fresh seafood for traditional Mexican fillings. The soft, juicy fish tacos with a tomato-and-pineapple sauce are particularly addictive. Lunch around $7.

Maha's Café (**F** B1)
→ *65-1148 Mamalahoa Hwy, Kamuela Tel. 885-0693 Daily 8am–4.30pm*
This friendly coffee shop is rightly famous for its fantastic poi pancakes with coconut syrup and endless cups of Kona coffee. You'll want to come back the next day for the papaya coffee cake and homemade banana bread, and won't be able to resist a takeaway lunch of fresh guava juice, honey-smoked *ahi* with *lilikoi* salsa and the irresistible macadamia nut shortbread cookies for dessert. Breakfast around $9.

Sam Choy's Kaloko (**F** B4)
→ *73-5576 Kauhola St, near Kailua-Kona Tel. 326-1545 Mon-Sat 6am–2pm; Sun 7am–2pm*
Sam Choy is one of Hawaii's favorite sophisticated Pacific Rim chefs, but this restaurant – which looks something like a reconstructed airplane hangar – is all casual, down-home, local-style cooking. Come early for Sam's enormous, delicious breakfasts, which can include soufflé-size heaps of fluffy scrambled eggs, mountains of fried rice, and thick coins of spicy, sweet Portuguese sausage. À la carte $15.

Café Pesto (**F** C2)
→ *Kawaihae Shopping Center, South Kohala Coast (between Kailua-Kona and Kamuela) Tel. 969-6640 Sun-Thu 11am–9pm (10pm Fri-Sat)*
A favorite of locals and tourists alike, this sunny restaurant serves up creative pizzas (the Pizza Luau is topped with *kalua* pork, sweet onions, and fresh pineapple), appetizers (Asian-flavored crabcakes with a honey-miso vinaigrette and

MAUNAKEA GALLERY

HulaBean
COFFEE

HULA BEAN COFFEE

PARKER RANCH STORE

cucumber salad), and fish-heavy, Pan-Asian-inspired entrees (like the wok-fired shrimp and scallops with cilantro and roasted macadamia nuts). The servings are generous, but save room for dessert. Entrées $22.

Merriman's (**F** A1)
→ *65-1227 Opelo Rd, Kamuela Tel. 885-6822 Mon-Fri 11.30am–1.30pm; Mon-Sun 5.30–9pm*
This breezy local favorite, which bills itself as 'Hawaiian Art Deco with a splash of French country', uses only ingredients grown by local farmers and cooperatives, and is well known for its succulent medallions of seared *ahi* and its burgers made from local grass-fed beef. Reservations advised. À la carte $25.

Koa House Grill (**F** B1)
→ *65-1144 Mamalahoa Hwy, Kamuela Tel. 885-2088 Daily 11.30am–2pm, 5.30–9pm*
Koa House Grill offers fresh fish and seafood, but it's their meat – meltingly tender filet mignon and steaks, *lilikoi*-glazed spareribs – that keeps this cheerful restaurant a local favorite. Like most of the restaurants in the area, Koa House relies upon locals, both as patrons and suppliers. À la carte $26.

Daniel Thiebaut (**F** A1)
→ *65-1259 Kawaihae Rd, Kamuela Tel. 887-2200 Mon-Fri 11.30am–2pm; daily 5.30–8.30pm*
Daniel Thiebaut's inventive cuisine – crabcakes topped with Hilo-grown sweet corn, a seared rare Napoleon of *ono* and wilted baby *bok choy* – manages to be surprising without sliding into cuteness or fussiness. The restaurant, which is housed in a modest wooden yellow structure, is always packed with locals and tourists alike. $30 prix fixe.

BAR

Huggo's on the Rocks (**F** B4)
→ *75-5828 Kahakai Rd, Kailua-Kona Tel. 329-1493 Daily 11.30am–late*
Popular and trendy beachside bar and club, and the younger sibling of the Huggo's seafood restaurant next door. Come here just before sunset. The small bar menu features fajitas, salads, sandwiches and tasty appetizers.

SHOPPING

Maunakea Gallery (**F** A1)
→ *65-1298 Kawaihae Rd, Kamuela Tel. 887-2244 Mon-Sat 10am–5pm*
You can buy any Hawaiiana or Pacifica you can think of at this beautiful treasure trove of a gallery, from high art (200-year-old etchings) to high camp (a 1950s plastic hula doll). Maunakea also sells contemporary koa furniture, retro-inspired rattan settees, pottery and posters, but they're renowned for their wide collection of Hawaiian prints. The gallery also ships worldwide, and the staff is knowledgeable and patient.

Dan De Luz Woods, Inc. (**F** B1)
→ *64-1013 Mamalahoa Hwy, Kamuela Tel. 885-5856 Mon-Sat 9am–5pm; sometimes open on Sun (call in advance)*
Fashioned from native hardwoods, Hawaiian lathe-turned bowls and calabashes make a special – and expensive – souvenir of the islands; prices for a bowl can run into the thousands. But there are all sorts of affordable bowls at master wood-carver Dan De Luz's studio-cum-showroom, including many under $100, and, in the back of the store, De Luz's own collection of his most treasured bowls, made from every kind of tropical wood imaginable.

Parker Ranch Store (**F** A1)
→ *Hwy 19, between Lindsey and Pukalani Roads, Kamuela Tel. 885-5669 Mon-Sat 9am–5.30pm (5pm Sun)*
After a visit to the ranch, step into this cheerful gift store, where you can purchase locally made lotions and jerky made from local cattle.

Hula Bean Coffee (**F** B5)
→ *75-5719 Alii Drive, Kailua-Kona Tel. 329-6152 Daily 7.30am–9.30pm*
The original outpost of this local company serves all variations of rich, dark Kona coffee, grown locally and ground fresh. Enjoy a cup (or two) and then have a few pounds – and some of the company's fab retro T-shirts and posters – mailed to your friends back home.

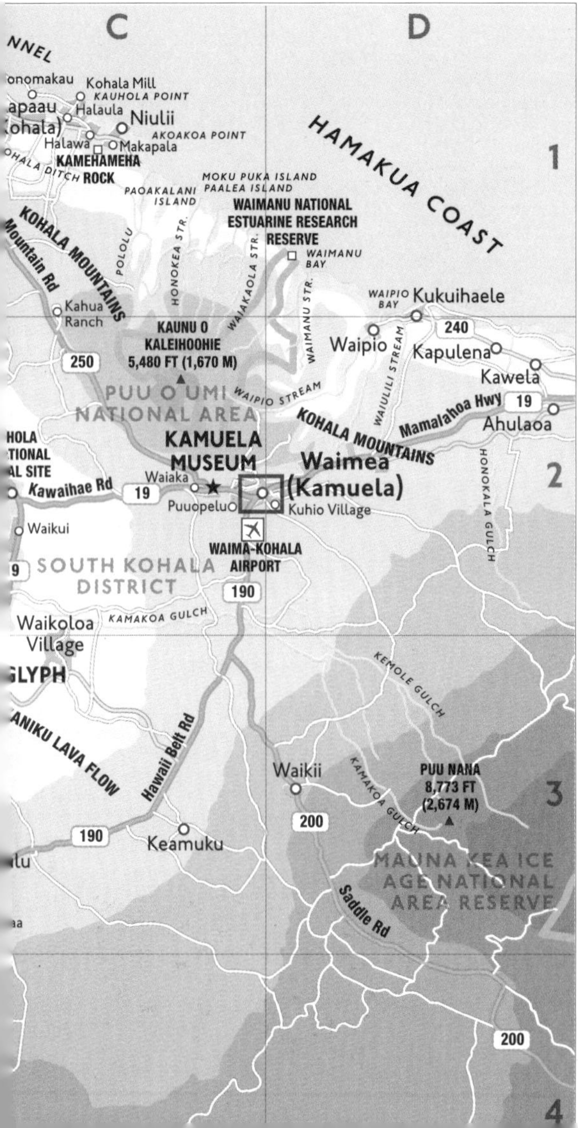
C
D
1
2
3
4
HAMAKUA COAST
Kohala Mill
KAUHOLA POINT
Halaula
Niulii
AKOAKOA POINT
Halawa
Makapala
KAMEHAMEHA ROCK
MOKU PUKA ISLAND
PAALEA ISLAND
PAOAKALANI ISLAND
WAIMANU NATIONAL ESTUARINE RESEARCH RESERVE
WAIMANU BAY
KOHALA MOUNTAINS
Mountain Rd
POLOLU
HONOKEA STR.
WAIAKAOLA STR.
WAIMANU STR.
WAIPIO BAY
Kukuihaele
Kahua Ranch
KAUNU O KALEIHOOHIE 5,480 FT (1,670 M)
240
Waipio
WAIULILI STREAM
Kapulena
Kawela
250
PUU O UMI NATIONAL AREA
WAIPIO STREAM
Mamalahoa Hwy
19
Ahulaoa
KAMUELA MUSEUM
Waimea (Kamuela)
HONOKALA GULCH
Kawaihae Rd
Waiaka
Puuopelu
Kuhio Village
Waikui
WAIMA-KOHALA AIRPORT
SOUTH KOHALA DISTRICT
190
Waikoloa Village
KAMAKOA GULCH
KEMOLE GULCH
Hawaii Belt Rd
Waikii
KAMAKOA GULCH
PUU NANA 8,773 FT (2,674 M)
200
Keamuku
MAUNA KEA ICE AGE NATIONAL AREA RESERVE
Saddle Rd

PUUHONUA O HONAUNAU

KONA COFFEE FARMS

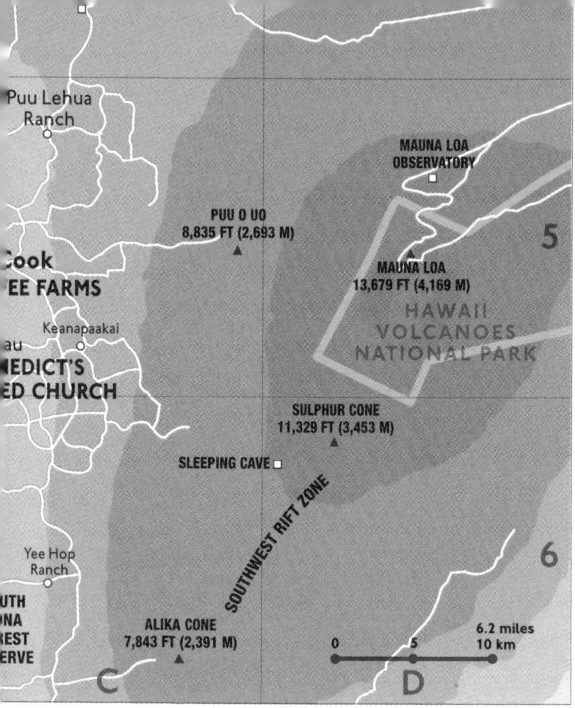

Puu Lehua
Ranch
MAUNA LOA
OBSERVATORY
PUU O UO
8,835 FT (2,693 M)
5
ook
EE FARMS
MAUNA LOA
13,679 FT (4,169 M)
HAWAII
VOLCANOES
NATIONAL PARK
Keanapaakai
au
EDICT'S
ED CHURCH
SULPHUR CONE
11,329 FT (3,453 M)
SLEEPING CAVE
SOUTHWEST RIFT ZONE
Yee Hop
Ranch
6
UTH
NA
EST
ERVE
ALIKA CONE
7,843 FT (2,391 M)
0
5
6.2 miles
10 km
C
D

ST BENEDICT'S PAINTED CHURCH

AHUENA HEIAU

oopoo Beach
nty Park (**F** B5)
outh of Kealakekua Bay
Captain Cook
oopoo may not look
pitable, with its many
croppings of slippery
s and stingy shred
beach, but past the
s, it offers some of the
nd's best snorkeling;
water teems with
el-colored fish.

honua O Honaunau
y of Refuge) (**F** B5)
onaunau, near Kailua-
a, off an unmarked road
k for directions
328-2288
y 7.30am–5.30pm
of Hawaii's most haunting sites, used to be home to a royal palace as well as several *heiaus*, or sacred temples, which were destroyed by foreign visitors and have been partially reconstructed here. 'City of Refuge' is something of a misnomer since this site offered redemption, not refuge, for the guilty; if you could slip past the fortified guards, you would be granted clemency. At the edge of this site is a stretch of crystal-clear water, as well as tidepools around which sea turtles swim lazy circles.

Captain Cook Monument (**F** B5)
The British explorer and seafarer Captain James Cook was the first Westerner to make contact with the islands, but his relationship with the islanders deteriorated, and he was killed at Kealakekua Bay in 1779. This monument in Cook's memory was established in 1884.

Kona Coffee Farms (**F** B5)
→ *Along Hwy 11, between Honalo and Ho'okena*
Kona coffee's rich, smoky flavor has won it countless fans, and many of the dozens of farms along this 20-odd-mile stretch of highway welcome visitors (and offer free samples). Coffee with as little as 10 percent Kona beans can be classified as Kona coffee, but here, you can buy 100 percent Kona coffee.

St Benedict's Painted Church (**F** B5)
→ *Off Hwy 160, east of Puuhonua O Honaunau*
This beautiful and unassuming wooden church was built and decorated between 1899 and 1904 by a Belgian priest. The interior trompe l'oeil is modeled after a Gothic cathedral in Burgos, Spain, and the ceiling is painted with long, graceful arcs of palm trees. Outside is a small cemetery set among extravagant blooming trees and bushes.

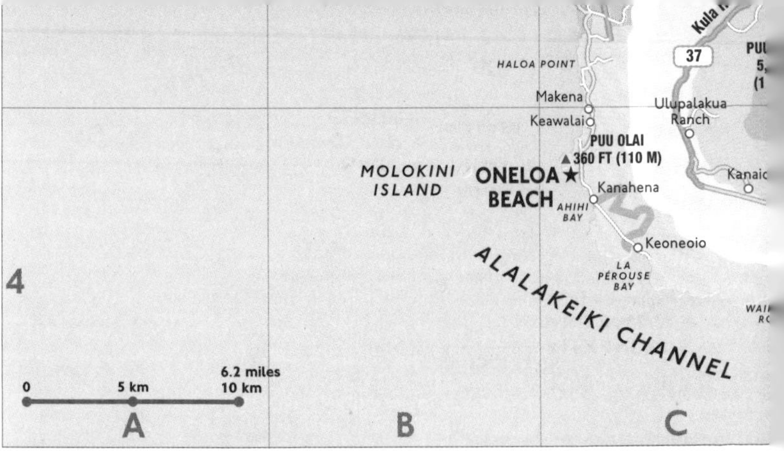
Kula
37
HALOA POINT
Makena
Keawalai
Ulupalakua Ranch
PUU OLAI
▲360 FT (110 M)
MOLOKINI ISLAND
ONELOA BEACH ★
Kanahena
Kanaio
AHIHI BAY
Keoneoio
LA PÉROUSE BAY
ALALAKEIKI CHANNEL
4
0
5 km
6.2 miles
10 km
A
B
C

ONELOA BEACH

KULA BOTANICAL GARDENS

ALEXANDER AND BAL

Piiholo Ranch (**G** B2)
→ *55 South Wakea Ave, in Kahului Tel. 357-5544 Tours offered Mon-Sat 8.30am and 10.30am*
Owned by the Baldwins, longtime Hawaii residents, this working ranch also offers visitors a taste of the upcountry *paniolo*'s life. The historically rich tours lead you around the lush grounds, speckled with koa trees, ferns and lazing cattle. Try to go when the ranch is conducting a cattle drive.

Road to Hana (**G** DE-2)
From Paia, take the famously blind and cork-screw turns of the 70 miles of Hana Highway. There you'll see some of the most gorgeous scenery on the island: great vistas, clusters of flowers, and green-furred mountains. There are gardens and nurseries along the way, but few real places to stop for amenities until Hana itself. The drive takes about three hours.

Haleakala Visitors' Center (**G** D3)
→ *11 miles from park entrance Tel. 572-4400 Daily dawn–3pm*
The steep drive up to Maui's 10,000-foot dormant volcanic centerpiece is one of the most fascinating anywhere; the terrain changes from tropics to prairie to tundra to woodlands. On the way up are any number of small flower farms, some specializing in protea flowers. Make sure to stop; many offer tours of the grounds and most can ship these oddly furry blooms, which make lovely and unusual dried bouquets.

Haleakala Crater (**G** E3)
Eight miles across, and shrouded in mist, it is as unlike Kilauea as you can imagine. Instead of heat and molten lava, the crater is a vast, pitted lunar landscape. The view is spectacular during sunrise. Several trails leave from the visitors' center and tak you into the crater. Whi walking about, keep ar out for the rare and prir silversword, or *ahinahi* large, curious frosted fc of a plant that can take decades to bloom. Alsc bring a sweater or light as Haleakala can get co

Baldwin Home (**G** A2)
→ *Front and Dickenson in Lahaina Tel. 661-326 Daily 10am–4pm*
Now a tourist town, hist Lahaina was once Haw capital under the reigns Kamehameha II and III. the first half of the 19th century, it was also an important whaling port,

PIIHOLO RANCH

THE ROAD TO HANA

HALEAKALA

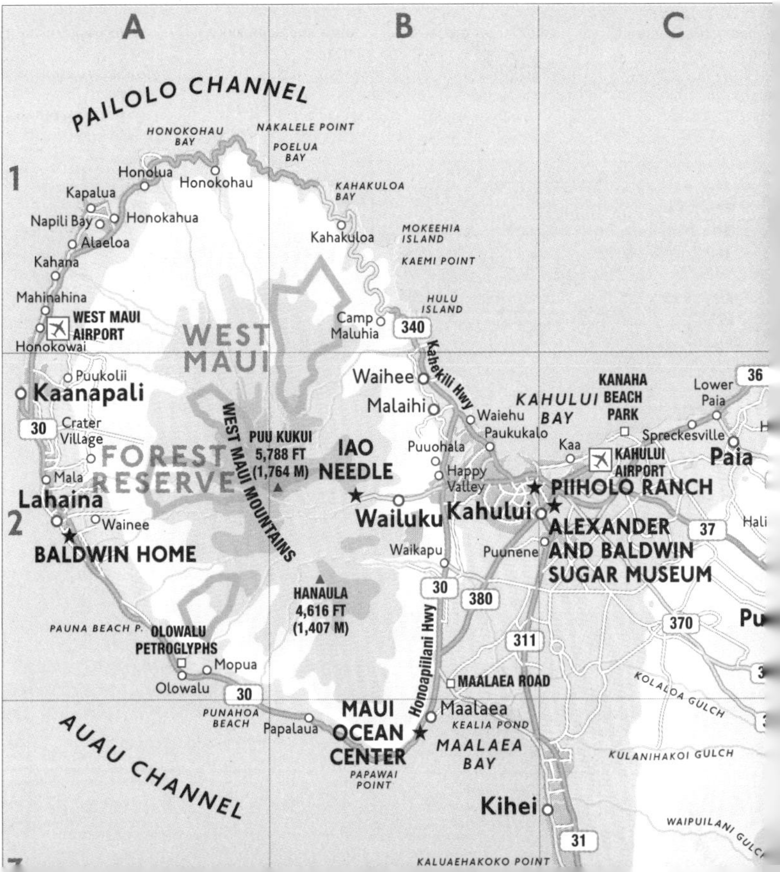
A
B
C
1
2
PAILOLO CHANNEL
AUAU CHANNEL
HONOKOHAU BAY
NAKALELE POINT
POELUA BAY
KAHAKULOA BAY
MOKEEHIA ISLAND
KAEMI POINT
HULU ISLAND
Honolua
Honokohau
Kapalua
Napili Bay
Honokahua
Alaeloa
Kahana
Kahakuloa
Mahinahina
WEST MAUI AIRPORT
Honokowai
Camp Maluhia
340
WEST MAUI
Puukolii
Kaanapali
Waihee
Kahekili Hwy
Malaihi
KAHULUI BAY
KANAHA BEACH PARK
Lower Paia
36
30
Crater Village
WEST MAUI MOUNTAINS
PUU KUKUI 5,788 FT (1,764 M)
IAO NEEDLE
Waiehu
Paukukalo
Puuohala
Kaa
KAHULUI AIRPORT
Spreckesville
Paia
FOREST RESERVE
Mala
Happy Valley
PIIHOLO RANCH
Lahaina
Wailuku
Kahului
ALEXANDER AND BALDWIN SUGAR MUSEUM
Wainee
37
Hali
BALDWIN HOME
Waikapu
Puunene
HANAULA 4,616 FT (1,407 M)
380
370
Pu
PAUNA BEACH P.
OLOWALU PETROGLYPHS
Honoapiilani Hwy
311
Mopua
Olowalu
MAALAEA ROAD
KOLALOA GULCH
PUNAHOA BEACH
Papalaua
MAUI OCEAN CENTER
Maalaea
KEALIA POND
MAALAEA BAY
KULANIHAKOI GULCH
PAPAWAI POINT
Kihei
WAIPUILANI GULCH
31
KALUAEHAKOKO POINT

If Waikiki is a tourist's kitsch paradise, Maui – all of Maui – is the luxe version. Tourists (not to mention work-wearied Honolulu-ites) flock to this island for its splendorous spas, sweeping vistas and excellent beaches. Like the Big Island, Maui is an island of extreme climates and terrains; you can spend a morning lazing on a pristine white-sand beach and the afternoon gazing at barren, snow-capped peaks from the summit of Haleakala. It's also a place of extreme social diversity, from the vacationers at the plush resorts to upcountry's hippie dropouts to the longtime Maui-ites whose families have called the island home for generations.

HALIIMAILE GENERAL STORE

HUI NO'EAU CENTER

RESTAURANTS

Sam Sato's (**G** B2)
→ *The Millyard, 1750 Wili Pa Loop, in Wailuku*
Tel. 244-7124
Mon-Sat 7am–2pm
An island institution, mainly for its saimin, which is garnished with confetti-like tossings of egg, green onions, and *char siu*, and its 'dry mein', a Maui special: saimin noodles sprinkled with bean spouts and green onions served with a dipping cup of clear broth on the side.
À la carte around $6.

Spices (**G** C3)
→ *2259 South Kihei Rd, in Kihei*
Tel. 891-8860
Breakfast: daily 7–11.30am; Lunch 11:30am–3pm; Dinner 5–10pm
Helmed by a French-Moroccan chef who came to the islands by way of Atlanta, this restaurant brings a Mediterranean flair to its interestingly meat-heavy (pork loin, lamb chops, steak) menu; try the distinctive Mediterranean chicken, which is made with the chef's homemade preserved lemons. Reservations advised. À la carte $20.

Haliimaile General Store (**G** D2)
→ *900 Haliimaile Rd, in Haliimaile*
Tel. 572-2666
Mon-Fri 11am–2.30pm, 5.30–9:30pm
This island favorite, located in a landmark 1926 converted storefront, produces imaginative, farm-fresh entrées for a packed house. Chef Beverly Gannon was one of the original parents of Hawaii regional cuisine, and has become something of an Alice Waters figure to this agriculturally rich and diverse area. Reservations advised.
À la carte around $30.

BARS

Roy's Kihei Bar and Grill (**G** C3)
→ *Piilani Village 303 Piikea Ave, in Kihei*
Tel. 891-1120
Daily 5.30–10pm

Roy's Kahana Bar and Grill (**G** A1)
→ *4405 Honoapiilani Hwy, in Kapalua*
Tel. 669-6999
Daily 5.30–10pm
Bars do abound on Maui (especially in Lahaina

AO KULA

HANA COAST GALLERY

TEDESCHI VINEYARD

and Kihei), but they tend to be either strictly touristy joints or unremarkable, sticky-tabled dives. So while Roy Yamaguchi's eponymous chain of upscale restaurants may seem tiresomely ubiquitous, they're probably your best bet for a good drink in elegant and fun surroundings. Join the lively mix of tourists and locals at the bar, where you can enjoy a couple of cocktails – not to mention some light and flavorful Euro-Asian *pupus* – and watch the equally memorable sunset.

SHOPPING

Maui Grown Market (**G** D2)
→ *914 Hana Hwy, in Haiku*
Tel. 572-1693
Daily 6.30am–6pm
Maui Grown Market has distinguished itself as both the last pit stop on the notoriously twisty road to Hana, but also as the only place in the state (at least!) where you can rent a dog for a day. Tourists homesick for their own canines stop here for boxed lunches (a sandwich, drink, chips, cookies and candy bar) and water, but also to borrow one of the many placid mutts lounging about, most of whom are good with children and all of whom will endure the road's nauseating hairpin turns with much more equanimity than their human companions. Just bring them back before closing.

Hui No'eau Visual Arts Center (**G** D2)
→ *2841 Baldwin Ave, in Makawao*
Tel. 572-6560
Daily 10am–4pm
In the past few years, this tiny ranching town has seen the birth of a half dozen new galleries. Hui No'eau, which hosts jewelry, glass, sculpture, ceramic, drawing and painting classes, among others, is the burgeoning art scene's nexus. There's also a lively mix of rotating exhibits and lectures, as well as a gift shop selling work by local artists.

Hana Coast Gallery (**G** F3)
→ *At the Hotel Hana-Maui at Hana Ranch, in Hana*
Tel. 248-8636
Daily 9am–5pm
This friendly gallery sells paintings, jewelry, furniture, paper sculptures and drawings, but what makes the visit worthwhile is its beautiful selection of luminous Hawaiian calabashes and bowls, including those by J. Kelly Dunn and world-renowned turner Ron Kent's wafer-thin, near-transluscent Norfolk Pine vessels.

Ono Organic Farms Star (**G** F3)
→ *Route 149, in Hana*
Tel. 248-7779
Call two or three days in advance to schedule a tour
One of Maui's many superlative organic farms, Ono Farms grows their own tropical fruits (papayas, rambutans, jackfruits, lychee and starfruits among them) and their own coffee. They'll ship anywhere.

Nanea Ao Kula (**G** D3)
→ *1100 Waipoli Rd, in Kula*
Tel. 878-3004
Gift shop 10am–4pm; tours 10am–1.30pm
It's almost impossible not to grow vegetation on Haleakala's lush slopes, and the road to the summit is dotted with dozens of small farms and plantations. One of the prettiest is this lavender farm, which ships dozens of delicious homegrown confections (lavender honey, lavender vinegar, lavender sugar, lavender tea) and bath products (soaps, lotions, bath salts) worldwide. The farm offers three different tours through its beautiful, relaxing grounds; make sure to reserve your spot in advance.

Ulupalakua Ranch and Tedeschi Vineyard (**G** C4)
→ *Hwy 37, in Ulupalakua*
Tel. 878-6058
Tasting room open daily 9am–5pm; tours 9.30am and 2.30pm
Originally owned by an ex-whaling captain, Ulupalakua is today home to the Tedeschi winery, which produces white, red, and rosé wines, as well as its own champagne. Make sure to try the popular Maui Blanc, a pineapple wine, and take a tour of the grounds, which are shaded by enormous old trees.

HALEAKALA HIKE

BALDWIN HOME

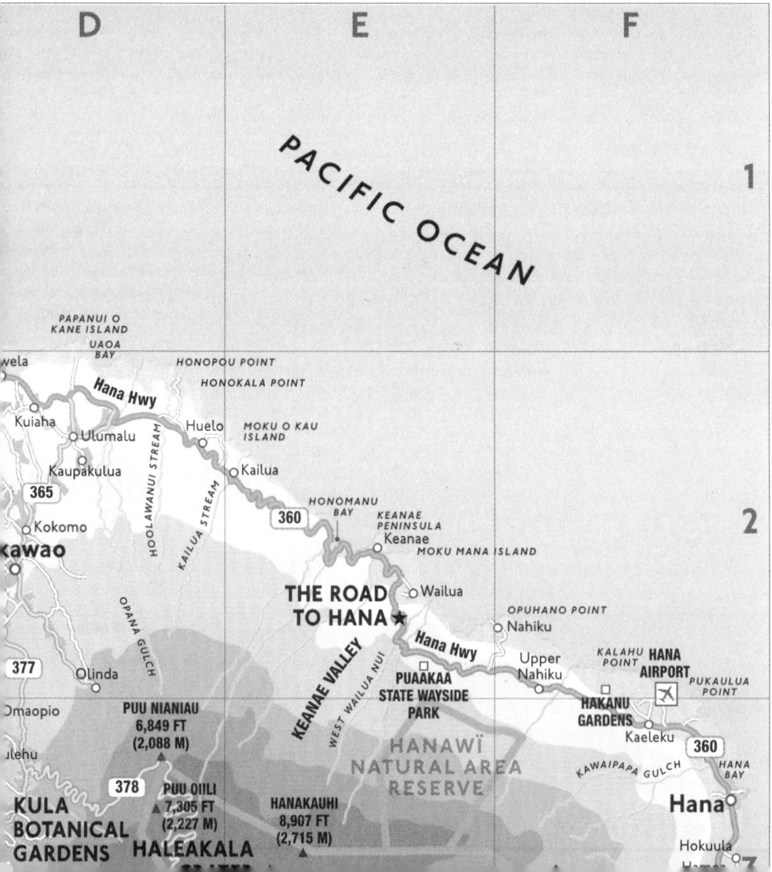
D
E
F
1
2
PACIFIC OCEAN
PAPANUI O KANE ISLAND
UAOA BAY
HONOPOU POINT
HONOKALA POINT
Hana Hwy
Kuiaha
Ulumalu
Huelo
MOKU O KAU ISLAND
Kaupakulua
Kailua
365
HOOLAWANUI STREAM
KAILUA STREAM
HONOMANU BAY
360
KEANAE PENINSULA
Keanae
Kokomo
MOKU MANA ISLAND
THE ROAD TO HANA
Wailua
OPANA GULCH
OPUHANO POINT
Nahiku
KEANAE VALLEY
WEST WAILUA NUI
Upper Nahiku
KALAHU POINT
HANA AIRPORT
PUKAULUA POINT
377
Olinda
PUAAKAA STATE WAYSIDE PARK
HAKANU GARDENS
PUU NIANIAU
6,849 FT
(2,088 M)
Kaeleku
HANAWĪ NATURAL AREA RESERVE
KAWAIPAPA GULCH
HANA BAY
378
PUU OIILI
7,305 FT
(2,227 M)
KULA BOTANICAL GARDENS
HALEAKALA
HANAKAUHI
8,907 FT
(2,715 M)
Hana
Hokuula

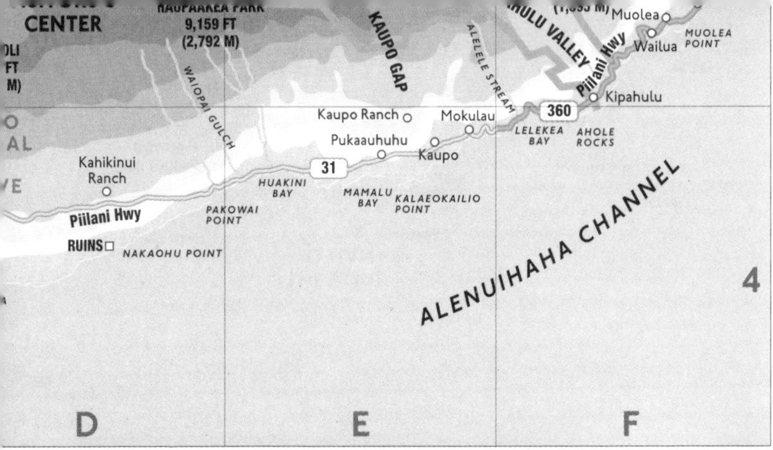
CENTER
9,159 FT
(2,792 M)
KAUPO GAP
ALELELE STREAM
Muolea
MUOLEA POINT
Wailua
Piilani Hwy
Kipahulu
WAIOPAI GULCH
Kaupo Ranch
Mokulau
360
LELEKEA BAY
AHOLE ROCKS
Pukaauhuhu
Kaupo
Kahikinui Ranch
31
HUAKINI BAY
MAMALU BAY
KALAEOKAILIO POINT
PAKOWAI POINT
Piilani Hwy
RUINS
NAKAOHU POINT
ALENUIHAHA CHANNEL
4
D
E
F

USEUM

MAUI OCEAN CENTER

IAO NEEDLE

acting sailors and stian missionaries. authentic landmark is lwin Home, which was e occupied by the stian missionary erend Dwight Baldwin, preached to native vaiians and sailors alike ne 1840s through 1860s.

ui Ocean Center (**G** B3)
xit 30 off Honoapiilani , in Maalaea Tel. 270- o Daily 9am–6pm
ell-edited aquarium, of many tropical fish and llife, some of them truly rre, plus a discovery l with mollusks, sea ins and sea cucumbers separate tanks for Hawaiian sea turtles and stingrays and eagle rays.

Alexander and Baldwin Sugar Museum (**G** C2)
→ *3957 Hansen Rd, in Kahului Tel. 871-8058 Mon-Sat 9.30am–4.30pm*
For years, sugar was Maui's primary crop, and although today most of the factories are closed, at evenings the air is still thick with the sticky-sweet scent of burning cane. Alexander and Baldwin was one of Maui's most important sugar companies, and here you can explore working models of sugar factory machinery, as well as exhibits about the immigrants who worked in the fields and who peopled the Hawaii of today.

Iao Needle (**G** B2)
→ *Iao Valley Rd, Iao Valley State Park, outside Wailuku*
From Iao Valley State Park, look up at the Iao Needle, a phallic, foliage-encrusted pinnacle jutting up from a high ridge. The 2,250-foot protrusion was once used as a natural altar. The valley itself was the location of a decisive, extremely bloody battle between the Maui army and Kamehameha the Great's troops in 1790.

Kula Botanical Gardens (**G** D3)
→ *Upper Kula Rd, ¾ mile from the Kula Hwy turnoff Tel. 878-6455 Mon-Sat 9am–4pm*
Gardening aficionados must stop by this 6-acre estate that is home to thousands of native and imported tropical trees and wonderful flowers: whorls of ferns, quilled proteas and pigtailed anthuriums dazzle the eye.

Oneloa Beach (**G** C4)
→ *Take the first turn off the road south of Makena*
Also known as Big Beach, with unbelievably blue water and a gorgeous, endless stretch of buff-colored sand. Be careful though; there is no reef here, so the waves can be murderous and the undertow fierce.

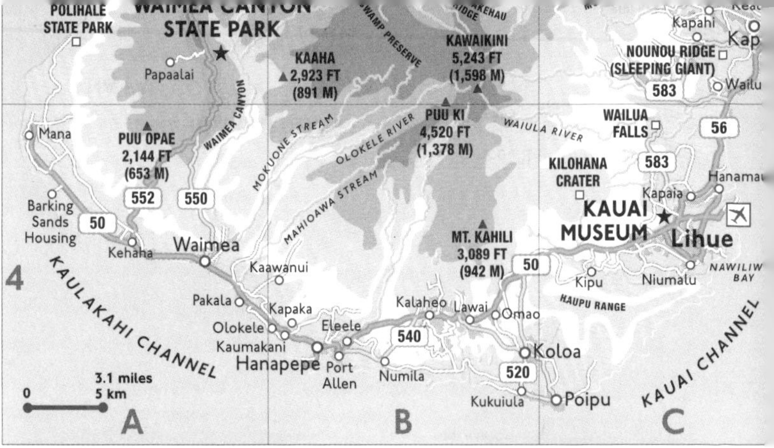

POLIHALE STATE PARK
WAIMEA CANYON STATE PARK
Papaalai
KAAHA
2,923 FT
(891 M)
KAWAIKINI
5,243 FT
(1,598 M)
Kapahi
NOUNOU RIDGE
(SLEEPING GIANT)
583
Wailu
Mana
PUU OPAE
2,144 FT
(653 M)
WAIMEA CANYON
MOKUONE STREAM
OLOKELE RIVER
PUU KI
4,520 FT
(1,378 M)
WAIULA RIVER
WAILUA FALLS
56
583
KILOHANA CRATER
Hanamau
MAHIOAWA STREAM
Kapaia
552
550
Barking Sands Housing
50
KAUAI MUSEUM
Lihue
Kehaha
Waimea
MT. KAHILI
3,089 FT
(942 M)
50
4
KAULAKAHI CHANNEL
Kaawanui
Kipu
Niumalu
NAWILIW BAY
Pakala
HAUPU RANGE
Kapaka
Kalaheo
Lawai
Omao
Olokele
Eleele
540
Kaumakani
Koloa
Hanapepe
Port Allen
Numila
520
KAUAI CHANNEL
3.1 miles
5 km
0
Kukuiula
Poipu
A
B
C

LIMAHULI GARDEN

KAUAI MUSEUM

NA PALI COAST

Lanai

Hulopoe Beach (H E4)
➔ *End of Manele Rd (Hwy 440), south of Lanai City*
Easily the island's best snorkeling, swimming, and diving spot, right below the Manele Bay Hotel, where you can sometimes see playful spinner dolphins.

The Munro Trail (H E4)
Take the trail (7 to 20 miles depending where you start) behind the Lodge at Koele or Manele Road, south of Lanai City; it takes you along the edge of Lanai's razorbacked hump. Munro, a New Zealander who lived in Hawaii during the 1920s, planted the area with hundreds of Norfolk Island and Cook Island pine seedlings. Today, in addition to these massive pines there is much wild flora and fauna: ferns, mesquite and guava trees, turkeys. On clear days, from the summit you can see Maui, Molokai, Kahoolawe, Hawaii and, if you squint, Oahu.

Garden of the Gods (H D3)
➔ *Polihua Rd, about 6 miles north of Lanai City*
The scattered rock formations here can appear as meaningful and mysterious as Easter Island's famous heads. This eerie spot is best visited during the brief twilight, when the rocks cast long, mesmerizing shadows and the light turns the dirt pink, blue and mustard.

Molokai

Kalaupapa (H D1)
➔ *Father Damien Tours*
Tel. 567-6171
Mon-Sat 7–10am, 2–8pm
In the 19th century, people with leprosy were exiled by Kamehameha V to this grim peninsula off Molokai's northern coast, left to die in the company of their fellow sufferers. In 1873, Father Damien, a Belgian Catholic priest, went to live among the lepers until he succumbed to the disease himself in 1889. A cure discovered in 1946, bu stigma surrounding the illness lingered. Today, colony is a place of raw beauty, a haunted outp nestled in Molokai's cl

Halawa Valley (H F1)
➔ *Take Maunaloa Hwy (Hwy 460) all the way ea*
A breathtaking sight is North Shore, dominate by giant, cloud-scrapin impossibly green cliffs. Visiting by air or boat is like glimpsing primeval unspoiled and majestic Hawaii. Halawa, the mo famous of the North Sh valleys, was an ancient thriving farming comm

HULOPOE BEACH

THE MUNRO TRAIL – THE NORTHERN END

THE MUNRO TR

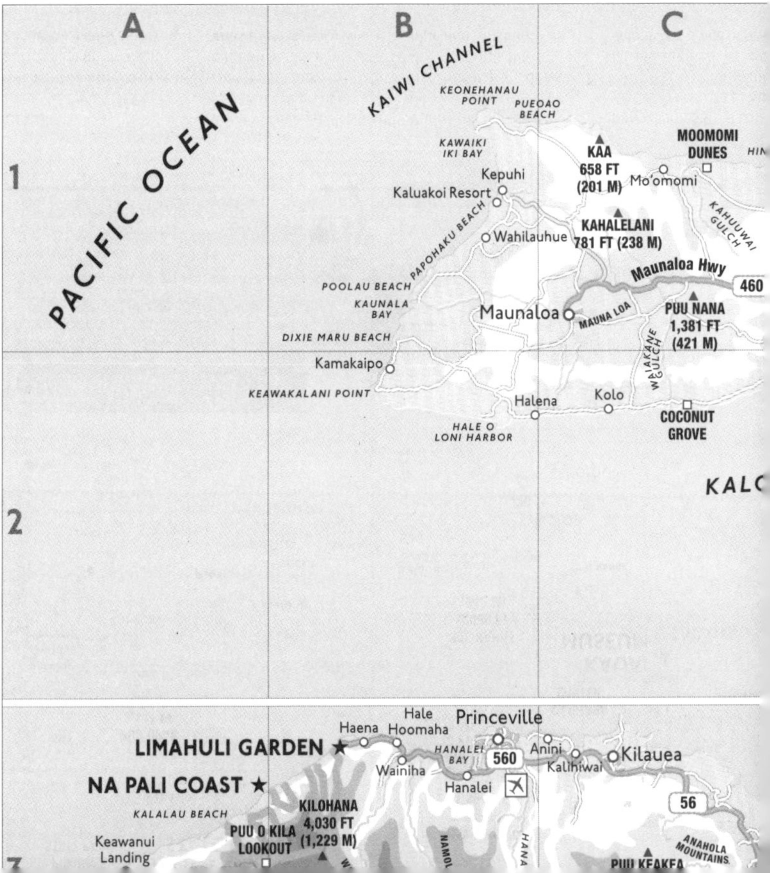
A
B
C
1
2
PACIFIC OCEAN
KAIWI CHANNEL
KEONEHANAU POINT
PUEOAO BEACH
KAWAIKI IKI BAY
KAA 658 FT (201 M)
MOOMOMI DUNES
Mo'omomi
Kepuhi
Kaluakoi Resort
PAPOHAKU BEACH
Wahilauhue
KAHALELANI 781 FT (238 M)
KAHUUWAI GULCH
Maunaloa Hwy
460
POOLAU BEACH
KAUNALA BAY
Maunaloa
MAUNA LOA
PUU NANA 1,381 FT (421 M)
DIXIE MARU BEACH
WAIAKANE GULCH
Kamakaipo
KEAWAKALANI POINT
Halena
Kolo
HALE O LONI HARBOR
COCONUT GROVE
KALC
Hale Hoomaha
Haena
Princeville
LIMAHULI GARDEN ★
HANALEI BAY
560
Anini
Kalihiwai
Kilauea
Wainiha
Hanalei
NA PALI COAST ★
56
KALALAU BEACH
KILOHANA 4,030 FT (1,229 M)
PUU O KILA LOOKOUT
Keawanui Landing
ANAHOLA MOUNTAINS
PUU KEAKEA

The popular image of Hawaii – sparkling beaches, floral-scented breezes, bikini-clad tourists – persists because so much of it is true; a visit to parts of the Big Island, Oahu and Maui confirms it all. But a visit to one of Hawaii's less-trafficked islands – Lanai, Kauai and especially Molokai – demands a certain readjustment. All three are spectacularly beautiful, but they have never achieved the glitter and swaggering urbanity of the other islands. And while it's easy to dismiss this trio as backwater colonials, each has had to overcome difficult histories and daunting challenges to carve out hard-won identities in the shadow of their luckier sisters.

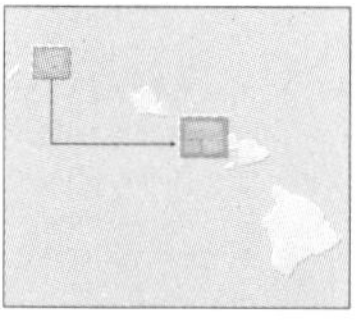

IHILANI DINING ROOM AT MANELE BAY HOTEL

LOTUS GALLER

LANAI

Mainly known as the seat of Hawaii's pineapple industry, it is the least populous of the Hawaiian islands.

Restaurants

Are few because there's only one town: Lanai City. **Coffee Works** *(604 Ilima St, Tel. 565-6962)* is perfect for fresh-roasted grounds and baked goods; **Blue Ginger Café** *(409 7th St, Tel. 565-6363)* for diner food with a local-Japanese twist; **Tanigawa's** *(419 7th St, Tel. 565-6537)* for down-home Japanese food.

The Formal Dining Room (**H** E3)
→ *The Lodge at Koele, Keomuku Rd, Lanai*
Tel. 565-7300
Dinner 6–9.30pm
This dining room is very earnest about its look and food – New American cuisine made with fresh seafood, poultry and vegetables – and is given stellar rankings by guests and critics alike. Reservations necessary. À la carte $42.

Ihilani Dining Room (**H** E4)
→ *Manele Bay Hotel, off Manele Rd (Hwy 440)*
Tel. 565-2296 Daily 6–9.30pm
One of the two fine-dining restaurants here, with lots of fresh seafood, fruits and vegetables and a fairly good wine list. Book ahead. Set menu around $85; with wine $125.

MOLOKAI

The antidote to the Hawaiian cliché some may have in mind (pampering hotels, luxury shopping and noisy restaurants), Molokai is all about stripped-down eco-tourism, haunting history and dramatic landscapes.

Restaurants

Kamuela's Cookhouse (**H** D1)
→ *Uwao and Farrington Aves, Kualapuu Tel. 567-9655*
Mon-Sat 6.30am–2.30pm; Sun 10am–3pm
A former farmhouse, it is Kualapuu's only eatery, a friendly greasy spoon, with generous mahi sandwiches, hamburgers and heaping breakfasts. À la carte $10.

Shopping

Saturday market (**H** D1)
→ *Ala Malama St, Kaunakakai*
Dawn until mid afternoon
A trip to Hawaii's farmers' markets is a humbling experience for even the most knowledgeable vegetable cognoscento. Farmers set up stalls banked with fruits and

KANEMITSU BAKERY

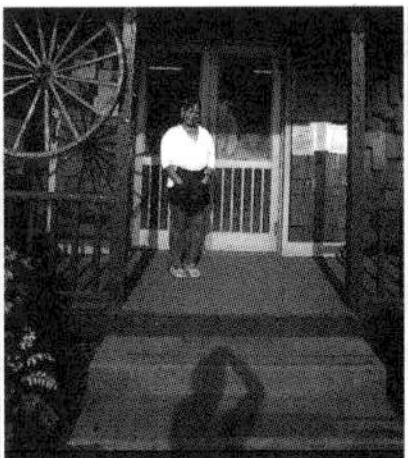

A COOKHOUSE IN MOLOKAI

LANAI CITY

vegetables both recognizable and not. Afterward, wander through tiny Kaunakakai, whose painted wooden storefronts will make you feel like you've stepped back in time.

Kanemitsu Bakery (**H** D1)
→ *79 Ala Malama St, Kaunakakai Tel. 553-5855 Wed-Mon 5.30am–6.30pm*
Aside from their famously soft, flavorful and faintly sweet loaves of bread (including taro and Portugese sweet bread), the bakery also makes a fantastic *lavosh*, which is addictive on its own but irresistible with a smear of *lilikoi* butter.

KAUAI

Thought to be home to the earliest Polynesian settlers, verdant, slow-paced, sleepy Kauai is also home to some world-class luxury resorts. Its real draw, however, is incredibly lush gardens and spellbinding cliffs, which lend the land its air of magic and mystery.

Restaurants

Hamura Saimin Stand (**H** C4)
→ *2956 Kress St, Lihue Tel. 245-3271 Mon-Thu 10am–11pm (midnight Fri-Sat; 9pm Sun)*
Saimin (a version of ramen noodles, topped with Spam or *char siu*) is Hawaii's favorite savory snack. Connoisseurs the islands over consider the saimin made at this tiny shack the best in the state. Also delicious *yakitori* and *yakiniku* (grilled chicken and beef, respectively). À la carte $5.

Beach House Poipu Restaurant (**H** C4)
→ *5022 Lawai Rd, Poipu Tel. 742-1424 Open nightly, lounge at 5pm. Dinner 6–9.30pm*

Roy's Poipu Bar and Grill (**H** C4)
→ *2360 Kiahuna Plantation Drive, Poipu Tel. 742-5000 Daily 5.30–9.30pm*
Two of Hawaii's most popular chefs, Jean-Marie Josselin and Roy Yamaguchi, have opened satellite restaurants in Poipu, which houses the island's most important condominium and luxury hotels, including the posh Kauai Hyatt Regency Resort and Spa. Reservations essential. À la carte for both about $26.

A Pacific Café (**H** C3)
→ *4-831 Kuhio Hwy, Kapaa Tel. 822-0013 Daily 5.30–9.30pm*
Jean-Marie Josselin's flagship Kauai restaurant is breezy, with colorful, overstuffed floral arrangements and rattan chairs. The food here is more Hawaii regional cuisine, with lots of fresh fish (try the flash-fried *tempura sashimi* when it's available) and desserts featuring lots of silky macadamia nuts. The service is as bright as the wine list. Reservations highly recommended. À la carte about $26.

Shopping

Unlike Maui, Oahu or the Big Island, Kauai isn't known for its shopping but for its fantastic vistas and landscapes, pleated cliffs and its rich history. However, luxury hotels tend to support a few upscale boutiques and gift shops. And Kauai's major tourist towns all have their own mini-malls – although the balance of quality to kitsch will vary wildly (and will usually be tipped toward the latter). Some of the more interesting include:

Hanalei Center (**H** B3)
→ *5-5161 Kuhio Hwy, Hanalei Tel. 826-7677*
Housed in an old schoolhouse, its shops sell all manner of knick-knacks and curiosities; **Kilohana Plantation** *(3-2087 Kaumualii Hwy, near Lihue)* has mainly local crafts; **Kinipopo Shopping Village** *(4-356 Kuhio Hwy, Kapaa)* features the Tin Can Mailman Bookstore, where you can pore over old maps and ephemera; and **Poipu Shopping Village** *(2360 Kiahuna Plantation Drive, Poipu)* has resort wear and accessories such as black pearl necklaces.

Lotus Gallery (**H** C3)
→ *At the Kong Lung Center, Lighthouse Rd, Kilauea Tel. 828-9898 Daily 10am–6pm*
This lively gallery sells a hodgepodge of Asian art and antiques, especially its beautiful selection of (mostly) South and Southeast Asian-inspired baubles, which glitter enticingly from behind the dark cabinets' glass doors.

Yellow Fish Trading Co (**H** B3)
→ *5-5016 Kuhio Hwy, Hanalei Tel. 826-1227 Daily 9.30am–9pm*
A fun and kitsch store, Yellow Fish stocks all manner of Elvis-era Hawaiiana, including aloha shirts, hula dolls and other memorabilia you never knew you needed.

GARDEN OF THE GODS

KALAUPAPA

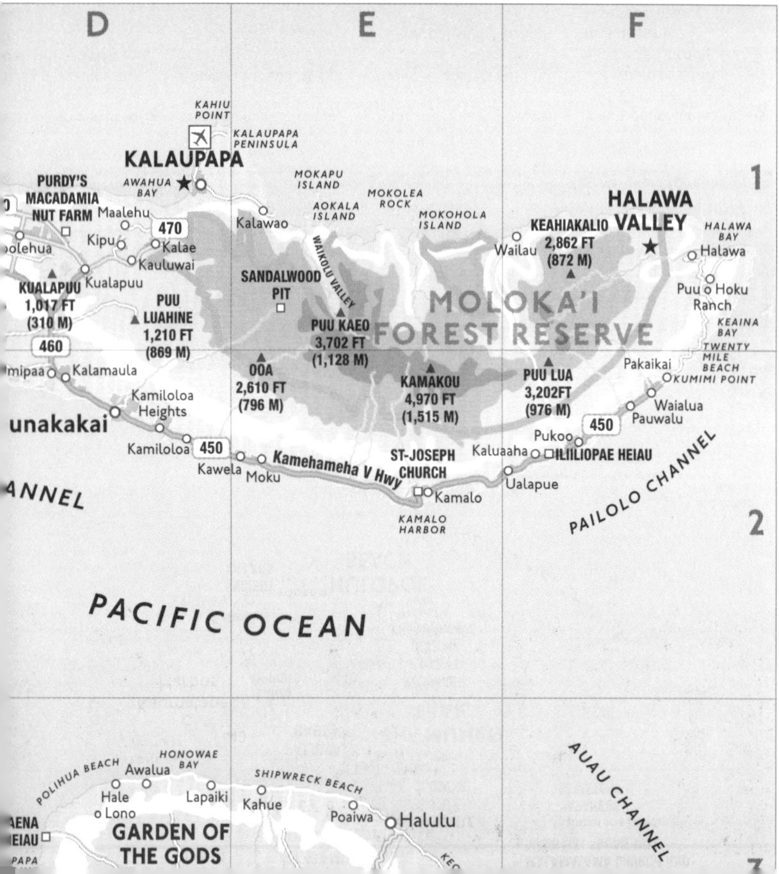

D
E
F
1
2
KAHIU POINT
KALAUPAPA PENINSULA
KALAUPAPA
AWAHUA BAY
PURDY'S MACADAMIA NUT FARM
Maalehu
470
Kipu
Kalae
Kauluwai
Kalawao
MOKAPU ISLAND
AOKALA ISLAND
MOKOLEA ROCK
MOKOHOLA ISLAND
WAIKOLU VALLEY
SANDALWOOD PIT
KUALAPUU 1,017 FT (310 M)
Kualapuu
PUU LUAHINE 1,210 FT (869 M)
PUU KAEO 3,702 FT (1,128 M)
OOA 2,610 FT (796 M)
KAMAKOU 4,970 FT (1,515 M)
PUU LUA 3,202FT (976 M)
MOLOKA'I FOREST RESERVE
HALAWA VALLEY
KEAHIAKALIO 2,862 FT (872 M)
Wailau
HALAWA BAY
Halawa
Puu o Hoku Ranch
KEAINA BAY
TWENTY MILE BEACH
Pakaikai
KUMIMI POINT
Waialua
Pauwalu
450
Pukoo
Kaluaaha
ILIILIOPAE HEIAU
Ualapue
ST-JOSEPH CHURCH
Kamalo
KAMALO HARBOR
Kamehameha V Hwy
Kawela
Moku
Kamiloloa
Kamiloloa Heights
Kalamaula
460
PAILOLO CHANNEL
PACIFIC OCEAN
POLIHUA BEACH
HONOWAE BAY
Awalua
Hale
Lono
Lapaiki
SHIPWRECK BEACH
Kahue
Poaiwa
Halulu
GARDEN OF THE GODS
AUAU CHANNEL

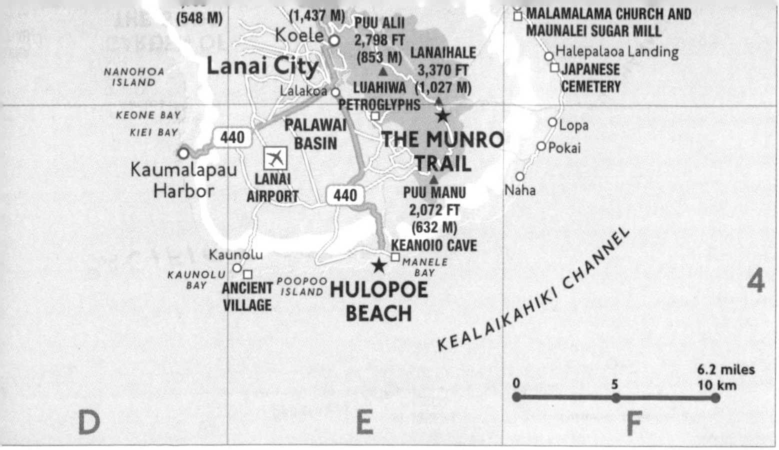
(548 M)
(1,437 M)
Koele
PUU ALII
2,798 FT
(853 M)
LANAIHALE
3,370 FT
(1,027 M)
MALAMALAMA CHURCH AND
MAUNALEI SUGAR MILL
Halepalaoa Landing
JAPANESE
CEMETERY
NANOHOA
ISLAND
Lanai City
Lalakoa
LUAHIWA
PETROGLYPHS
KEONE BAY
KIEI BAY
440
PALAWAI
BASIN
THE MUNRO
TRAIL
Lopa
Pokai
Naha
Kaumalapau
Harbor
LANAI
AIRPORT
440
PUU MANU
2,072 FT
(632 M)
KEANOIO CAVE
MANELE
BAY
Kaunolu
KAUNOLU
BAY
ANCIENT
VILLAGE
POOPOO
ISLAND
HULOPOE
BEACH
KEALAIKAHIKI CHANNEL
4
0
5
6.2 miles
10 km
D
E
F

WAIMEA CANYON STATE PARK

HALAWA VALLEY

was destroyed in 1946 huge tsunami. Today, ners are working to ore the Hawaiian way fe.

uai

ai Museum (H C4)

428 Rice St, in Lihue 245-6931 Mon-Fri 1–4pm; Sat 10am–4pm

s modest little museum an offhand charm with nderful examples of litional wooden abashes and feather , as well as a collection ncient Hawaiian aponry. A gift shop sells oks about Hawaiian tory and customs, ally made crafts and beautiful lauhala mats, which can be shipped.

Limahuli Garden (H B3)

→ On Kuhio Hwy, about 6 miles west of Hanalei
Tel. 826-1053
Tue-Fri, Sun 9.30am–4pm

Only a 15-acre round of this 1,000-plus-acre natural preserve is open to the public, but it is full of wonders, including a terraced steppe where taro is grown in the traditional manner; there is wild yellow ginger, stalks of *awapuhi* (whose flowers make a natural shampoo), spindly mountain apple trees bearing their sweetish, slightly mealy fruit, and a fantastic view from the top of the hill.

Na Pali Coast (H A-B3)

On Kauai's northwest shore, between Kee and Polihale, loom the famous 2,000-foot cliffs, or Na Pali. Seeing these cliffs – its difficult terrain precludes any visit by vehicle or certainly by foot – with their massive, undulating pleats, is an indescribable experience. Long ago, ancient Hawaiians used to live in some of these valleys, protected against all other society by the area's sheer inaccessibility. Boat tours and helicopters can take you close to the area's pounding waterfalls and silent, haunted lands, but nature has never seemed so inconquerable as it does here.

Waimea Canyon State Park (H A3)

→ Take Kaumaualii Hwy at Waimea until Waimea Canyon Drive

Another of Kauai's fantastic natural wonders, it is over 10 miles long and over 3,000 feet deep. But unlike the Grand Canyon's harsh redness, Waimea Canyon is a dazzling display of color and texture, sprouts of greenery and, in the distance, rushing, ceaseless waterfalls.

WAIPIO VALLEY, BIG ISLAND

SPOUTING HORN, KAUAI

Hawaii abounds with hotels to fit every budget, but try to spend at least one night at a luxury resort. Some are almost baroque in their ostentation, but the finer ones – especially on Maui and the Big Island – can be transporting, with heavenly golf courses, pampering spas, gorgeously landscaped grounds, magnificent beaches and, in some cases, a fine collection of works by contemporary artists (better, sometimes, than what you'll see in museums). Except where otherwise stated, prices given are for a double room with bathroom. Hotel tax (11.41 percent) is not included. Advance reservations are highly recommended.

♦ Spa ⚐ Golf course

OAHU

Honolulu

Kahala Mandarin Oriental (C C6)
→ *5000 Kahala Ave*
Tel. 739-8888
www.mandarin-oriental.com/kahala/
An elegant, luxurious hotel tucked away in one of Honolulu's most exclusive residential neighborhoods. From the lobby to the spa to the shops, this hotel is first rate. The food is also very good, as is the beach and the 26,000-sq-ft lagoon, where you can frolic with dolphins. From $295. ♦

The Halekulani (A B2)
→ *2199 Kalia Rd*
Tel. 923-2311
www.halekulani.com
One of the most distinguished hotels in Hawaii and certainly the best in Waikiki. The unflashy, old-world service is excellent, as is the food. The new spa is a must. From $325. ♦

The Sheraton Moana Surfrider (A C2)
→ *2365 Kalakaua Ave*
Tel. 922-3111
www.moanasurfrider.com
This beautifully restored plantation-style hotel near the end of the Waikiki strip doesn't feel as claustrophobic as many of the neighborhood's hotels. From $270.

Hilton Hawaiian Village (A A1)
→ *2005 Kalia Rd*
Tel. 949-4321
www.hilton.com
The ultimate in cheerful Waikiki kitsch, with lots of classes and activities for guests of all ages. There are four pools and the beach, of course. $189. ♦

W Hotel at Diamond Head (A C4)
→ *2885 Kalakaua Ave*
Tel. 922-1700
www.starwood.com/whotels
There are glamorous young guests and a remarkably attractive staff at this W hotel. Separated from Waikiki proper by a chain of some of the neighborhood's best beaches, it has a jazzy, laid-back cool and an excellent bar. From $265.

New Otani Kaimana Beach Hotel (A C4)
→ *2863 Kalakaua Ave*
Tel. 922-9404
www.kaimana.com
Efficient, unflashy hotel perched on Sans Souci, one of Hawaii's best beaches, with a peaceful, picturesque location across from Kapiolani Park, 2 miles from Diamond Head. A very good bargain. $140.

Ilima Hotel (A C2)
→ *445 Nohonani St*
Tel. 923-1877 www.ilima.com
Basic, small, conveniently located and tucked away behind the neon façade of Waikiki. Studios from $129; suites from $179.

Marriott Ihilani Resort and Spa at Ko Olina (D B6)
→ *92-1001 Olani St, in Kapolei Tel. 679-0079*
www.ihilani.com
Locals and tourists alike love this off-the-beaten-track spot (23 miles west of Waikiki), as well as its very affordable spa. It's a nice reprieve from the crush of Honolulu (and yet the city's only minutes away). From $354. ♦ ⚐

Turtle Bay Resort (D D1)
→ *57-091 Kamehameha Hwy, Kahuku Tel. 293-8811*
www.turtlebayresort.com
This sprawling old favorite of a hotel provides a great escape from Honolulu. The new 21 Degrees North restaurant is also quite good, and the bodysurfing is often excellent. From $280. ♦ ⚐

Street names, monuments and places to visit are listed alphabetically. The references following each entry allow you to situate it in one or more of the eight geographical areas (**A**, **B**, **C**, etc.) presented in the guide.

WAIMEA BEACH, BIG ISLAND

DOWNTOWN HONOLULU

KILAUEA LIGHTHOUSE, NORTH KAUAI

period-inspired. From $145.

Garden Island Inn (**H** C4)
→ *3445 Wilcox Rd, Kalapaki Beach, Lihue, on Kauai*
Tel. 648-0154
www.gardenislandinn.com
The low-slung Garden Island Inn has clean, bright, simple rooms with lots of thoughtful details (a coffee-maker with fresh coffee, a microwave oven). A wild, untamed garden surrounds the hotel. From $75.

The Lodge at Koele (**H** E3)
→ *Lanai City, on Lanai*
Tel. 565-7300
www.lanai-resorts.com
Styled as an English country manor and set among thickets of tall, scraggly pines, this intimate hotel is a favorite of honeymooners, outdoorsmen (ask about the 4x4 adventure vacation package), and weary Honoluluans, who come for a quick getaway. Excellent golf course. From $375.

Manele Bay Hotel (**H** E4)
→ *Manele Bay, on Lanai*
Tel. 565-7700
www.lanai-resorts.com
The Lodge's seaside sister property is also beloved by golfers, who flock to its challenging course on the cliffs overlooking Hulopoe Bay. With a spa, great food, and a private, clean beach. From $375.

Hotel Lanai (**H** E3)
→ *828 Lanai Ave, Lanai City, on Lanai Tel. 565-7211*
www.hotellanai.com
Built by James Dole in 1923 as housing for Dole Plantation executives, this nicely renovated, lovely inn is known for its Cajun-inspired food and charm; it's a favorite with visiting Oahuans. Rooms from $105 (with breakfast).

Hotel Molokai (**H** D2)
→ *P.O. Box 1020, Kaunakakai, on Molokai*
Tel. 553-5347
www.hotelmolokai.com
A sleepy hotel perfectly in tune with the island's laid-back but genuine hospitality. There's a pool and a restaurant; the staff will help you arrange tours to Kalaupapa or various outdoor activities. Simple and attractive. From $85.

Sheraton Molokai Lodge and Beach Village (**H** C1)
→ *100 Maunaloa Hwy, Maunaloa, on Molokai*
Tel. 660-2824
www.sheraton-molokai.com
This deliberately rustic hotel bills itself as an adventure resort and Hawaii's best experiment in eco-tourism. The Lodge is an upscale hotel while Kaupoa Beach Village is a series of simple canvas bungalows. Together, the complex, which is private, stripped-down but still elegant, is a wonderful retreat. $275.

TOP GOLF COURSES

Big Island Four Seasons Hualalai, Kaupulehu-Kona. Jack Nicklaus-designed 18-hole course. *www.fourseasons.com*
Big Island Mauna Kea Beach Hotel, Kohala Coast; 18-hole course designed by Robert Trent Jones, Sr. *www.princeresortshawaii.com*
Maui Ritz-Carlton, Kapalua Three 18-hole courses designed by A. Palmer, B. Crenshaw and B. Coore. *www.ritzcarlton.com*
Kauai Princeville Resort, Princeville; 27- and 18-hole courses designed by Robert Trent Jones, Jr. *www.princeville.com*
Kauai Kauai Marriott Resort, Lihue. Two 18-hole courses by Jack Nicklaus. *www.marriott.com*
Lanai Manele Bay Hotel, Manele Bay. Another Jack Nicklaus-designed, fantastic 18-hole course, The Challenge. *www.lanai-resorts.com*

TOP FIVE SPAS

Oahu Halekulani Hotel, Honolulu (456 rooms; *www.halekulani.com*)
Oahu Marriott Ihilani Resort and Spa at Ko Olina, Kapolei (387 rooms, 36 suites; *www.ihilani.com*)
Big Island Four Seasons Hualalai, Kaupulehu-Kona (212 rooms, 31 suites; *www.fourseasons. com*)
Big Island Mauna Lani Resort, Kohala Coast (345 rooms, 5 bungalows *www.maunalani.com*)
Maui Four Seasons Resort Maui at Wailea, Wailea (305 rooms, 75 suites; *www.fourseasons.com*)

WINDSURFING

IOLANI PALACE CREST, HONOLULU

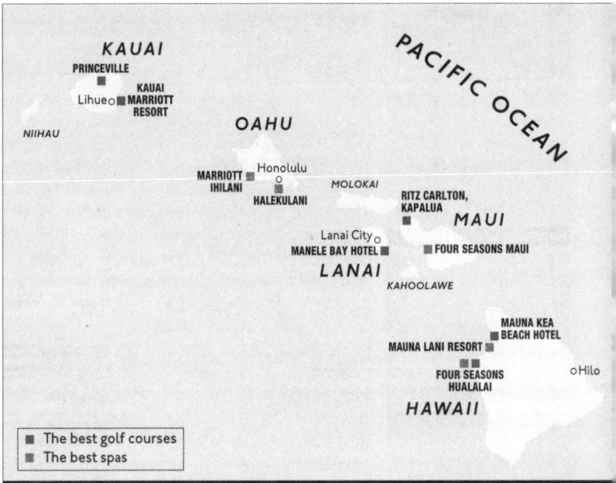

KAUAI
PACIFIC OCEAN
PRINCEVILLE
Lihue
KAUAI MARRIOTT RESORT
NIIHAU
OAHU
Honolulu
MARRIOTT IHILANI
HALEKULANI
MOLOKAI
RITZ CARLTON, KAPALUA
MAUI
Lanai City
MANELE BAY HOTEL
FOUR SEASONS MAUI
LANAI
KAHOOLAWE
MAUNA KEA BEACH HOTEL
MAUNA LANI RESORT
FOUR SEASONS HUALALAI
Hilo
HAWAII
The best golf courses
The best spas

HAWAII'S BEST SPAS AND GOLF COURSES

adviser. From $375.

The Old Wailuku Inn at Ulupono (**G** B2)
→ *2199 Kahookele St, Wailuku Tel. 244-5897*
www.mauiinn.com
A well-regarded inn in quiet, lush Wailuku. Elegant, wide *lanai* and comfortable rooms – true old-Hawaii style. From $120 (with breakfast).

Kaanapali Beach Hotel (**G** A2)
→ *2525 Kaanapali Pkwy, Lahaina Tel.661-0011*
www.kbhmaui.com
This low-slung, likable, down-to-earth resort is one of Hawaii's best values – there's easy beach access, a pool as well as lots of on-site activities (including a nightly hula show). The rooms are bland but clean. Interesting package deals. From $169.

Hana and Upcountry

Kula Lodge (**G** D3)
→ *RR1, Box 475, Kula Tel. 878-1535*
www.kulalodge.com
A rustic chalet high on the slopes of Haleakala outfitted with wood-burning fireplaces and a very decent restaurant. In the morning, the air tastes delicious. From $115–$175.

Hotel Hana-Maui (**G** F3)
→ *Hana Hwy, Hana Tel. 248-8211*
www.hotelhanamaui.com
Hawaii's first boutique resort, the Hana-Maui has recently been given an overhaul. Set among pines on a bluff overlooking the sea, it looks a little like a very sophisticated summer camp – though much more charming. From $295.

Heavenly Hana Inn (**G** F3)
→ *P.O. Box 790, Hana Tel. 248-8442*
www.heavenlyhanainn.com
Lovely, tranquil Japanese-style inn, complete with a tea and meditation rooms. Rooms have *o-furos*, and there's a garden banked with yellow bamboo. Asian or Western-inspired breakfast. From $185.

LANAI, MOLOKAI, KAUAI

Hyatt Regency Kauai (**H** B4)
→ *1571 Poipu Rd, Koloa, on Kauai Tel. 742-1234*
www.kauai.hyatt.com
This newly renovated, massive 5-acre hotel has white-sand beaches (better for surfing than swimming), a golf course, man-made saltwater lagoons and splashing waterfalls. From $395.

Princeville Resort (**H** B3)
→ *5520 Ka Haku Rd, Princeville, on Kauai Tel. 826-9644*
www.princeville.com
Kauai's most luxurious hotel, located on one of the island's best beaches. The Princeville (252 rooms) also has two spectacular, rolling golf courses, a spa and an enticing, oft-photographed sparkling eternity pool. From $425.

Kauai Marriott Resort and Beach Club (**H** C4)
→ *Kalapaki Beach, 3610 Rice St, Lihue, on Kauai Tel. 245-5050*
www.marriott.com
Another golfer's paradise. The decor of the Kauai Resor isn't particularly inspiring, but the beautiful, multipurpose Kalapaki Beach is. There's also an almost embarrassingly large pool. From $329.

Waimea Plantation Cottages (**H** A4)
→ *9400 Kaumualii Hwy, no 367, west of Waimea, on Kauai Tel. 338-1625*
www.aston-hotels.com
Unusual hotel in the midst of a verdant coconut grove. You can sleep in a restored plantation cottage or in the spacious manager's house. The structural integrity of the cottages has been retained and most of the decor is